Tort Law
2012–2013

D1513218

Routledge
Taylor & Francis Group

LONDON AND NEW YORK

Eighth edition published 2012
by Routledge
2 Park Square, Milton Park, Abingdon, Oxon OX14 4RN

Simultaneously published in the USA and Canada
by Routledge
711 Third Avenue, New York, NY 10017

Routledge is an imprint of the Taylor & Francis Group, an informa business
© 2012 Routledge

First edition published by Cavendish Publishing Limited 1997
Seventh edition published by Routledge 2010

British Library Cataloguing in Publication Data
A catalogue record for this book is available from the British Library

ISBN: 978-0-415-68344-9 (pbk)
ISBN: 978-0-203-31148-6 (ebk)

Typeset in Rotis
by RefineCatch Limited, Bungay, Suffolk

Printed and bound in Great Britain by
TJ International Ltd, Padstow, Cornwall

Contents

Table of Cases

Table of Statutes

Statutory Instruments

European Legislation

How to use this book

Welcome to this new edition of Routledge Tort Lawcards. In response to student feedback, we've added some new features to these new editions to give you all the support and preparation you need in order to face your law exams with confidence.

Inside this book you will find:

■ NEW tables of cases and statutes for ease of reference

■ Revision Checklist

We've summarised the key topics you will need to know for your law exams and broken them down into a handy revision checklist. Check them out at the beginning of each chapter, then after you have the chapter down, revisit the checklist and tick each topic off as you gain knowledge and confidence.

Sources of law

1

Primary legislation: Acts of Parliament	■
Secondary legislation	■
Case law	■
System of precedent	■
Common law	■
Equity	■
EU law	■
Human Rights Act 1998	■

■ Key Cases

We've identified the key cases that are most likely to come up in exams. To help you to ensure that you can cite cases with ease, we've included a brief account of the case and judgment for a quick aide-memoire.

HENDY LENNOX v GRAHAME PUTTICK [1984]

Basic facts

Diesel engines were supplied, subject to a *Romalpa* clause, then fitted to generators. Each engine had a serial number. When the buyer became insolvent the seller sought to recover one engine. The Receiver argued that the process of fitting the engine to the generator passed property to the buyer. The court disagreed and allowed the seller to recover the still identifiable engine despite the fact that some hours of work would be required to disconnect it.

Relevance

If the property remains identifiable and is not irredeemably changed by the manufacturing process a *Romalpa* clause may be viable.

■ Companion Website

At the end of each chapter you will be prompted to visit the Routledge Lawcards companion website where you can test your understanding online with specially prepared multiple-choice questions, as well as revise the key terms with our online glossary.

You should now be confident that you would be able to tick all of the boxes on the checklist at the beginning of this chapter. To check your knowledge of Sources of law why not visit the companion website and take the Multiple Choice Question test. Check your understanding of the terms and vocabulary used in this chapter with the flashcard glossary.

■ Exam Practice

Once you've acquired the basic knowledge, you'll want to put it to the test. The Routledge Questions and Answers provides examples of the kinds of questions that you will face in your exams, together with suggested answer plans and a fully-worked model answer. We've included one example free at the end of this book to help you put your technique and understanding into practice.

QUESTION 1

What are the main sources of law today?

Answer plan

This is, apparently, a very straightforward question, but the temptation is to ignore the European Community (EU) as a source of law and to over-emphasise custom as a source. The following structure does not make these mistakes:

■ in the contemporary situation, it would not be improper to start with the EU as a source of UK law;

■ then attention should be moved on to domestic sources of law: statute and common law;

■ the increased use of delegated legislation should be emphasised;

■ custom should be referred to, but its extremely limited operation must be emphasised.

ANSWER

European law

Since the UK joined the European Economic Community (EEC), now the EU, it has progressively but effectively passed the power to create laws which are operative in this country to the wider European institutions. The UK is now subject to Community law, not just as a direct consequence of the various treaties of accession passed by the UK Parliament, but increasingly, it is subject to the secondary legislation generated by the various institutions of the EU.

Negligence

1

NEGLIGENCE

Negligence forms the largest area of tort. In essence, negligence is a breach of a legal duty to take care of another which then results in loss or damage to the claimant. This breaks down into four components which must be proven by the claimant in order to establish negligence:

- The claimant must be owed a **duty of care**

- There must have been a **breach of duty**

- The breach of duty must have **caused** damage to the claimant

- The damage suffered by the claimant must not have been too **remote**.

Negligence is concerned with duty, breach, causation and remoteness. Each of these components will now be covered in turn.

DUTY OF CARE

DUTY SITUATIONS

The tests for determining the existence of a duty of care have changed. Prior to 1932, there were numerous incidents of liability for negligence but there was no connecting principle formulated which could be regarded as the basis of all of them. These were referred to as 'duty situations'.

THE NEIGHBOUR PRINCIPLE

The first attempt to create a rationale for all the discrete duty situations was made by Brett MR in *Heaven v Pender* [1883], but the most important formulation of a general principle is that of Lord Atkin in *Donoghue v Stevenson* [1932]. This is known as the 'neighbour principle':

> You must take reasonable care to avoid acts or omissions which you can reasonably foresee are likely to injure your neighbour. Who, then, in law is my neighbour? The answer seems to be – persons who are so closely and directly affected by my act that I ought reasonably to have them in contemplation as being so affected when I am directing my mind to the acts or omissions which are called into question.

THE 'TWO STAGE' TEST

The 'neighbour principle' is a test based on reasonable foresight of harm and is a very wide concept. It needed further refining.

In the 1970s, there were attempts to extend it by defining it as a general principle. In *Home Office v Dorset Yacht Co Ltd* [1970], Lord Reid said, '[the neighbour principle] ought to apply unless there is some justification or valid explanation for its exclusion'. This led to Lord Wilberforce's 'two stage' test in the case of *Anns v Merton LBC* [1977]:

> First, one has to ask whether ... there is a sufficient relationship of proximity ... in which case a *prima facie* duty arises. Secondly, if the first question is answered affirmatively, it is necessary to consider whether there are any policy considerations which ought to negative, or to reduce or limit the scope of the duty.

THE 'THREE STAGE' TEST

Lord Wilberforce's general principle in *Anns* soon came in for heavy criticism. This began with Lord Keith in *Governors of the Peabody Donation Fund v Sir Lindsay Parkinson & Co Ltd* [1984] when he said that, in addition to proximity, the court must decide whether it is 'fair, just and reasonable' to impose a duty of care.

The case of *Murphy v Brentwood District Council* [1990] marked the death knell for the 'two stage' test by overruling *Anns*. *Murphy* talked of adopting an 'incremental' approach to determining the existence of a duty of care. The most recent formulation of the principle comes from *Caparo Industries plc v Dickman* [1990].

> ❱ CAPARO INDUSTRIES PLC v DICKMAN [1990]
>
> Basic facts
> The appellants had undertaken the annual audit of a public company following the regulations laid out in the Companies Act 1985. The respondents were members of the company and had relied on the accounts to make a successful bid to take over the company. The respondents alleged that the accounts had been prepared negligently and their reliance on them had caused them a

loss as a result. The House of Lords had to decide whether the appellants owed the respondents a duty of care in the preparation of the accounts.

Relevance

When assessing whether a duty of care was owed the courts will take into account the following criteria (the 'three stage test'): i) reasonable foreseeability of harm; ii) proximity of relationship; iii) whether it would be fair, just and reasonable to impose a duty.

The reaction against the 'two stage' test was primarily focused on the fact that it created a massive extension to the tort of negligence. The 'incremental' approach avoids such an increase; instead, the tort of negligence is developed by analogy with existing cases. Any novel type of situation would have to show that it is analogous to an existing situation where a duty is owed and that it would be just, fair and reasonable to impose a duty of care in the circumstances.

POLICY CONSIDERATIONS

Policy plays a vital role in determining the existence of a duty of care. It can be defined as the departure from established legal principle for pragmatic purposes. Cases such as *Donoghue v Stevenson* and *Anns* consider policy expressly, whereas the approach followed in *Caparo* and *Murphy* is to consider policy impliedly and merge it in to other considerations such as 'proximity' and whether it is 'fair, just and reasonable' to impose a duty.

WHAT ISSUES OF POLICY ARE COMMONLY RAISED?

1   To allow a claim would open the 'floodgates' and expose the defendant to an indeterminate liability.

The courts are always keen to limit liability to a determinate amount and to a determinate class of persons. For example, in *Weller & Co v Foot and Mouth Disease Research Institute* [1965], the claimants were auctioneers who lost money on account of being unable to hold their auctions as a result of the defendant's negligence in allowing the foot and mouth virus to escape, which led to restrictions on the movement of cattle. It was said by the court that their damage was 'foreseeable', but so was the damage to 'countless other enterprises'. It would have been equally foreseeable that cafés or newsagents in the market town would also lose money. The burden on one defendant would be insupportable and policy had to act to limit liability.

2 The imposition of a duty would prevent the defendant from doing his job properly.

This leads to a class of what have been termed 'protected parties' – persons who enjoy immunity from suit:

- judges and witnesses in judicial proceedings enjoy immunity on grounds of 'public policy';

- barristers and solicitor-advocates. Lawyers used to enjoy immunity from suit concerning their conduct of cases in court: *Rondel v Worsley* [1967]. However, this case was overruled by the House of Lords in *Hall v Simons* [2000]. Lord Steyn commented that public policy was not immutable, and had changed since 1969. The court emphasised that an advocate's primary duty is to the court, and that performing this duty could never amount to negligence in the conduct of the client's case.

There is a public policy immunity for the carrying out of public duties by public bodies, unless that public body has assumed a responsibility to the individual. It is thought that to impose a duty in this situation would interfere with the way in which public bodies carry out their tasks. The immunity originates with the case of *Hill v Chief Constable of West Yorkshire* [1988]. The mother of the last victim of the Yorkshire Ripper sought to sue the police for negligence in failing to apprehend him earlier. There was found to be no special relationship between the police and the individual victim and consequently no duty could arise. It was felt that to impose a duty would be damaging to police operations. They would deploy their resources defensively on the basis of how they could best avoid civil liability, rather than on the basis of their professional judgment. The police had a duty towards the public as a whole.

The European Court of Human Rights in *Osman v UK* [1998] deprecated the idea of a 'blanket immunity' for the police from negligence actions – especially when police failings had led to a fatality. However, the English courts have subsequently insisted that *Hill* does not create a blanket immunity; rather, the fear of 'defensive policing' is one policy factor militating against a duty of care in novel actions brought against the police. The House of Lords applied *Hill* in *Brooks v Metropolitan Police Commissioner* [2005] in which the witness to a murder suffered post-traumatic stress disorder following his treatment by the police.

However, the police may be liable where there is a special relationship between the police and an informant (*Swinney v Chief Constable of Northumbria* [1996]). The police do not have a blanket immunity; there are other considerations of public policy which also carry weight. In *Swinney* Hirst LJ gave examples such as the need to protect springs of information, to protect informers, and to encourage them to come forward without an undue fear of the risk that their identity will become known to the suspect or to his associates. The facts of the case were that the claimant passed on to the police certain information concerning the unlawful killing of a police officer. The suspect was known to be violent. The informant requested that contact with her be made in confidence. The document containing the information supplied, together with the informant's name, was left in an unattended police car. The vehicle was broken into and the suspect obtained the document. It was arguable that a special relationship existed. But, in *Swinney v Chief Constable of Northumbria (No 2)* [1999], it was held that a duty of care was owed to an informant to take reasonable steps to preserve his confidentiality. However, in the circumstances, there had been no *breach* of that duty.

In *Van Colle v Chief Constable of Hertfordshire* [2007] the Court of Appeal was asked to consider whether the police were under a positive obligation to protect a witness' life under the Human Rights Act 1998 (Convention Art 2 'right to life' and the Art 8 'right to a private and family life') when they did not owe a duty to do so under the common law. The Court of Appeal held that where the police were aware of a real and immediate threat to the life of the witness, under Art 2 they had been in breach of a duty to take preventative measures to protect his life in failing to do so.

In the absence of such exceptional circumstances, an immunity did not arise in *Welton v North Cornwall District Council* [1996]. An environmental health officer, acting on behalf of a local authority, negligently required the owner of food premises to undertake extensive works to comply with the Food Act 1990. It was argued that the officer exercised a police or quasi-police function and there should be an immunity. This was rejected as the officer had assumed responsibility and, hence, a duty of care was owed.

The same public policy immunity for the discharge of public duties, unless responsibility had exceptionally been assumed to a particular defendant, also applies to the Crown Prosecution Service (*Elguzouli-Daf v Comr of Police of the Metropolis* [1995]) and the fire brigade (*Church of Jesus Christ of Latter Day Saints (Great Britain) v Yorkshire Fire and Civil Defence Authority* [1996]; *John Munroe (Acrylics) Ltd v London Fire and Civil Defence Authority* [1997]; *Nelson Holdings Ltd v British Gas plc* [1997]). However, a distinction was made between a positive act of negligence for which there would be liability on the part of the fire brigade and a negligent omission for which there would be no liability in *Capital Counties plc v Hampshire County Council* [1997]. A fire officer at the scene of the accident had ordered that a sprinkler system be switched off in a burning building. The result was that the fire spread and caused more damage.

In *Kent v Griffiths* [2000], the Court of Appeal held that an ambulance service, having answered an emergency call and promised to send an ambulance, came under a duty of care to do so. The court drew an analogy with a casualty department in a hospital, which owes a positive duty to treat those who enter its doors. It also seems that there was detrimental reliance upon the ambulance service's promise, in that the claimant could have tried to reach the hospital by alternative means had the undertaking not been made.

Phelps v Hillingdon London Borough Council [2000] concerned the negligence of educational psychologists employed by local authorities. The House of Lords held that, although it might not be possible to sue the authorities directly for the negligent organisation of their education departments, it was possible to sue the psychologists as they had assumed responsibility to the dyslexic children. (Even though the local authorities would have to pay the damages, in the end, through the doctrine of *vicarious liability* where an employer is held liable for torts committed by his employees.)

In *Z v UK* [2001], however, the European Court of Human Rights held, contrary to its decision in *Osman*, that there was no breach of Art 6(1) of the European Convention on Human Rights when an English court held that there was no duty of care owed by a local authority on public policy grounds. As the court explained, in the absence of duty there can be no tort, and therefore the claimant simply had no 'right' which required determination by an independent tribunal (as Art 6(1) requires).

3 It is against public policy to claim that you should not have been born, see *McKay v Essex AHA* [1982].

In *McFarlane v Tayside Health Authority* [1999], the House of Lords held that a doctor was not liable for the costs of bringing up a healthy child, born as a result of a negligently performed vasectomy. The court held that to allow such a claim would imply that the costs of bringing up the child outweighed the joys and benefits accruing to the parents and to society in general, and that this would offend the sanctity of life.

In *Rees v Darlington NHS Trust* [2003], the majority of a seven-man House of Lords refused to reconsider their Lordships' earlier unanimous decision in *McFarlane*. A child, even if unwanted, could not be regarded as a financial burden. However, a 'conventional award' of £15,000 was made, to represent the damage to the claimant's freedom to limit the size of her family, which the negligent performance of the sterilisation operation had brought about.

4 The courts will not impose a duty where there is an alternative system of compensation.

See *Hill v Chief Constable of West Yorkshire* [1988], where compensation was payable under the Criminal Injuries Compensation Scheme.

5 Constitutional relationship between Parliament and the courts.

The courts are reluctant to impose a duty where none existed before, as they see this as the constitutional role of Parliament. See Brooke LJ in *Hunter v British Coal Corporation* [1998].

The issue of the existence of a duty will arise only in novel cases or where it is sought to overrule an existing precedent against liability. This is referred to as a 'notional duty' and looks at the question from an abstract level. In most cases it will be a question of fact whether the defendant owes the claimant a duty of care on the particular facts of the case. This is referred to as a 'duty in fact'. The existence of that particular duty is not in issue; what is in issue is whether a duty is owed in that particular case.

PARTICULAR ASPECTS OF THE DUTY OF CARE

PHYSICAL INJURY

The meaning of the term 'proximity' varies according to who is using the term, when it is being used and the type of injury that has been suffered. As far as

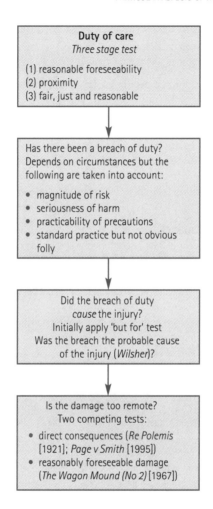

Duty of care
Three stage test

(1) reasonable foreseeability
(2) proximity
(3) fair, just and reasonable

Has there been a breach of duty?
Depends on circumstances but the
following are taken into account:

- magnitude of risk
- seriousness of harm
- practicability of precautions
- standard practice but not obvious
  folly

Did the breach of duty
cause the injury?
Initially apply 'but for' test
Was the breach the probable cause
of the injury (*Wilsher*)?

Is the damage too remote?
Two competing tests:

- direct consequences (*Re Polemis*
  [1921]; *Page v Smith* [1995])
- reasonably foreseeable damage
  (*The Wagon Mound (No 2)* [1967])

physical injury is concerned, the courts will readily hold the parties to be proximate and, for this type of injury, proximity really equates to foreseeability.

However, the House of Lords has held in *Marc Rich & Co AG v Bishop Rock Marine Co Ltd* [1995] that, even in cases of physical damage, the court had to consider not only foreseeability and proximity but also whether it was fair, just and reasonable to impose a duty.

In *Sutradhar v NERC* [2006] the House of Lords had to consider whether NERC was responsible to the Bangladeshi people (affected by drinking water contaminated by arsenic) when they had been commissioned by the Overseas Development Agency to test the local water for minerals that might be harmful to fish. NERC had not been asked, nor did they, test the water for arsenic. The House of Lords found that there must be proximity in the sense of a measure of control and responsibility for the potentially dangerous situation. In this instance there was no relationship between the parties such that the defendant was under a duty to the claimant to ensure that the water was safe to drink.

STAGES OF NEGLIGENCE

The third requirement of 'fair, just and reasonable' was lacking in *Mulcahy v Ministry of Defence* [1996]. The claimant was a soldier serving with the British Army in the Gulf War. He was injured and his hearing was affected when his gun commander negligently ordered a gun to be fired. Two of the components of a duty of care – foreseeability and proximity – were found to be present. However, taking into account the circumstances, including the position and role of the alleged tortfeasor and relevant policy considerations, it was not fair, just and reasonable to impose a duty.

Another example of the application of the *Caparo* test can be seen in *West Bromwich Albion Football Club v El-Safty* [2006]. A football club brought an action against a consultant surgeon for their financial losses arising from his negligence in prescribing treatment to one of their players. The Court of Appeal decided that although the claimant had paid for the treatment of the player (resulting in a degree of foreseeability and proximity existing between them and the defendant), it would not be fair, just and reasonable to impose a duty to the claimant because such a duty might conflict with the surgeon's primary duty to care for his patient (the player).

An unusual case of negligence causing physical injury is *Revill v Newbery* [1996]. The claimant, who was a trespasser and engaged in criminal activities, was attempting to break into a brick shed on the defendant's allotment. The defendant poked a shotgun through a small hole in the door and fired, injuring the claimant. The defendant was found to be negligent and had exceeded the level of violence justified in self defence. The claimant, however, was found to be two-thirds contributorily negligent.

In *Marc Rich*, Lord Steyn drew a distinction between 'directly inflicted' and 'indirectly inflicted' physical loss. He said that the law would more readily impose liability for the former than for the latter. The defendants unsuccessfully attempted to rely on this distinction in *Perrett v Collins* [1998]. One of the defendants had inspected a light aircraft and certified that it was airworthy. The other defendant was the certifying authority. They were held to owe a duty of care to the claimant, who was a passenger injured in a test flight. The Court of Appeal said that the distinction was more relevant to economic loss and was not germane to physical injury. The test would be applied in novel categories and did not apply to established categories of liability for personal injury.

RESCUERS

Rescuer as claimant

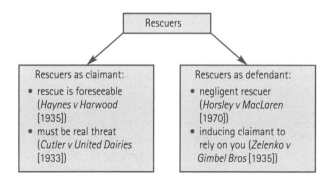

The law does not oblige a person to undertake a rescue unless the parties are in a special relationship, but the courts are favourably disposed to someone who does attempt a rescue and is injured in the process. Like physical injury, the courts require very little more than foreseeability before they hold the parties proximate.

The courts have held that where the defendant has negligently created a situation of danger, it is foreseeable that someone will attempt a rescue and it will not be possible for the defendant to argue *volenti non fit injuria* (that is, that the rescuer consented to the risk of injury) or that the rescuer's act constitutes a *novus actus interveniens*: *Haynes v Harwood* [1935]; *Baker v TE Hopkins & Son Ltd* [1959].

As far as rescuers are concerned, the courts are quick to regard someone intervening in a crisis as being foreseeable and impose few conditions in declaring the parties proximate. However, there must be a real threat of danger, see *Cutler v United Dairies (London) Ltd* [1933] in which the claimant attempted a rescue when no one was in a situation of danger and was consequently not owed a duty.

However, even if the victim was not in actual danger, the defendant will owe a duty if the rescuer's perception of danger was a reasonable one, see *Ould v Butler's Wharf Ltd* [1953].

The duty owed to a rescuer is independent from that owed to the accident victim. The defendant may, therefore, owe a duty to the rescuer where none is owed to the accident victim, see *Videan v British Transport Commission* [1963].

If someone negligently imperils himself or his property, it is foreseeable that there may be an attempt at a rescue and a duty of care will arise on the part of the accident victim. This includes a duty of care to a professional rescuer, such as a fire-fighter (*Ogwo v Taylor* [1987]).

Rescuer as defendant

Although rescuers are often held to be owed a duty, there are situations where a rescuer himself can owe a duty to the accident victim:

1 Where the rescuer by his conduct in commencing a rescue deters or prevents others from attempting a rescue, on the principle of 'detrimental reliance', see *Zelenko v Gimbel Bros* [1935].
2 There is Canadian authority for saying that where a rescuer worsens the condition of the accident victim, then the rescuer becomes liable to the accident victim, see *Horsley v MacLaren* [1970].
3 There is no duty at large to help someone in need of urgent assistance. However, when an ambulance service accepts a 999 call, a duty will be owed if the patient is identified by name and address.

OMISSIONS

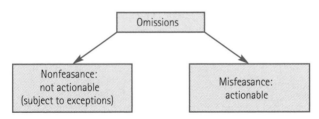

The law makes a distinction between misfeasance and nonfeasance. There is liability for the former but not for the latter. In other words, there is liability for doing something carelessly that causes damage, but there is no liability for omissions. A can watch B drown in an inch of water and incur no legal liability, unless A stands in a special relationship to B. However, if you start off a chain of events and then omit to do something, for example, begin driving a car and then omit to brake, with the result that you knock someone down, then there will be liability.

LIABILITY FOR ACTS OF THIRD PARTIES

Similarly, you cannot be held liable for the acts of third parties, unless there is a special relationship with that third party. In *P Perl (Exporters) Ltd v Camden LBC* [1983], thieves gained entry into the defendants' flat and then were able to break into the claimant's property. It was accepted that the damage was foreseeable but there was no obligation on the part of the defendants to prevent the harm from occurring.

Perl was followed in *King v Liverpool City Council* [1986]. Here, the defendants left their property vacant and unprotected, with the result that vandals gained entrance and damaged the claimant's flat. The defendants were held not to be responsible for the acts of the vandals. What particularly troubled the court was the question of what would be the extent of a defendant's obligation if he was obliged to protect his property. Would it have to be put under 24-hour guard?

In *Smith v Littlewoods Organisation Ltd* [1987], it was held that the defendant could be responsible for the acts of third parties if 'special circumstances' existed as follows:

- 'special relationship' between claimant and defendant;

- source of danger negligently created by the defendant and reasonably fore-seeable that third parties would interfere;

- the defendant had knowledge or means of knowledge that a third party had created or was creating a risk of danger on his property and failed to take reasonable steps to abate it.

On the facts of *Littlewoods*, the damage was not reasonably foreseeable, so the defendants were not liable. There was a difference in approach between the judges in *Littlewoods*; Lord Goff saw the intervention of a third party as a *novus actus interveniens* which 'breaks the chain of causation'. On the other hand, Lord Mackay saw the question not in terms of remoteness and causation but in terms of fault. He felt that a third party intervention does not absolve the defendant from liability but, in most cases, the chances of harm being caused by a third party are slim; therefore it is not reasonable to expect the defendant to take precautions against the harm occurring.

Lord Goff's view was followed by the Court of Appeal in *Topp v London Country Bus (South West) Ltd* [1993]. An employee of the defendant bus company habitually left his bus unlocked with the key in the ignition. After a short interval, a relief driver would drive the bus away. On the day in question, the relief driver failed to turn up and some time later the bus was stolen by joy riders who knocked down and killed the claimant's wife. The Court of Appeal held that no duty of care arose. Arguably, if Lord Mackay's test had been used then the claimant would have succeeded, as the trial judge had found the defendant's actions to be careless.

NERVOUS SHOCK OR PSYCHIATRIC INJURY

TYPES OF CLAIMANT IN NERVOUS SHOCK CASES

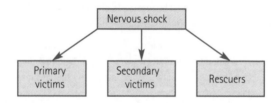

The courts have been slow to allow claims for nervous shock unless they are coupled with physical injury to the claimant. There are many criteria that the claimant must satisfy before there is liability for causing nervous shock through negligence.

NERVOUS SHOCK

	Primary victim	Secondary victim
What is regarded as being foreseeable?	Physical injury; psychiatric injury need not be foreseen	Psychiatric injury
Policy limitations	No	Yes

PRIMARY VICTIMS

The law of negligence relating to nervous shock makes an important distinction between primary and secondary victims. Primary victims are those who have been directly involved in the accident and are within the range of foreseeable physical injury. In the case of secondary victims, who are not within the range of foreseeable physical injury, control mechanisms are put in place to limit the number of claimants to avoid an opening of the floodgates. These principles are derived from a decision by the House of Lords in *Page v Smith* [1995].

> ### ▶ PAGE v SMITH [1995]
>
> Basic facts
> The claimant suffered from Chronic Fatigue Syndrome (Post Viral Fatigue Syndrome) which is considered to be a psychiatric injury by the law. The claimant was physically uninjured in a collision between his car and a car driven by the defendant but his condition became chronic and permanent as a result of the accident. Secondary victims are required to show that injury by way of nervous shock had to be foreseeable (*Bourhill v Young* [1942]; *King v Phillips* [1953]). In *Page v Smith*, the collision was relatively minor and nervous shock was not foreseeable. Nevertheless, the claimant recovered damages as a result of the foreseeability of physical injury, even though the claimant was not actually physically injured.

> Relevance
> There is no distinction between physical and psychiatric illness for primary victims.

In *Page v Smith*, Lord Lloyd felt that to inquire whether the claimant was actually physically injured introduces hindsight into the question of foreseeability, which has no part to play with primary victims, although hindsight was a legitimate consideration with secondary victims. Lord Lloyd also felt that there was no justification for introducing a distinction between physical and psychiatric illness, at least as far as primary victims are concerned.

DISTINCTION BETWEEN PRIMARY AND SECONDARY VICTIMS

Primary victims	Secondary victims
No policy control mechanisms to limit the number of claimants	Policy control mechanisms to limit claimants
Foreseeability of physical injury	Foreseeability of injury by way of nervous shock
Issue of foreseeability considered prospectively	Issue of foreseeability considered with hindsight
No distinction between physical or psychiatric injury	Distinction between physical and psychiatric injury
	Foreseeability judged by reference to whether a person of normal fortitude would have suffered a recognisable illness

Lord Keith, in a dissenting judgment, felt that the injury had to belong to a class or character that was foreseeable.

In *Rothwell v Chemical & Insulating Co Ltd* [2007] a former asbestos worker claimed that following his exposure to asbestos he had feared developing a serious asbestos-related disease in the future to such an extent that he had suffered from depression and anxiety as a result. Where the exposure to asbestos had caused no physical damage to the claimant's health, the Court of Appeal held that there was no evidence that a person of reasonable fortitude would have developed a mental illness under these circumstances and so found the employer not to be liable. This decision was appealed as one of a number that were jointly considered in *Grieves v FT Everard & Sons Ltd* [2007]. The House of Lords reiterated that it was not reasonably foreseeable that the creation of a risk of an asbestos-related disease would cause psychiatric illness to a person of reasonable fortitude.

In *Hunter v British Coal Corporation* [1998], Brooke LJ identified three categories of 'primary victim':

- those who fear physical injury to themselves;

- rescuers of the injured;

- those who believe they are about to be, or have been, the involuntary cause of another's death or injury.

However, in *Frost v Chief Constable of South Yorkshire* [1999], police officers had suffered nervous shock while on duty, in rescuing the victims of a disaster caused by negligence for which their employer was responsible. The House of Lords held that their status either as employees of the defendant or as rescuers did not make them primary victims. They had to satisfy the same test for all primary victims: were they within the zone of physical injury?

On the other hand, the House approved the success of the claim in *Walker v Northumberland County Council* [1995], where a social worker suffered a nervous breakdown when chronically overworked by his employer. (Guidelines were given on the extent of this employers' duty in *Sutherland v Hatton* [2002].) In *W v Essex County Council* [2000] the House of Lords held that it was arguable that parents could be primary victims, where they felt themselves to blame for the sexual abuse of their natural children by a foster child, who had been negligently placed with them by the defendant council. The parents had not personally been at risk of abuse.

SECONDARY VICTIMS

Medically recognised psychiatric illness or disorder
Before there can be liability in the case of secondary victims, there must be a medically recognised psychiatric illness or medical disorder; there is no liability for emotional distress or grief unless this leads to a recognisable medical condition. These have been held to include:

■ depression (*Chadwick v British Transport Commission* [1967]);

■ personality change (*McLoughlin v O'Brian* [1982]);

■ post-traumatic stress disorder (*Hale v London Underground* [1993]).

It was held in *Hicks v Chief Constable of South Yorkshire* [1992] that there could be no claim for the terror suffered immediately before death in the knowledge that death was imminent.

An abnormally sensitive claimant will be unable to recover unless a person of 'normal' fortitude would have suffered.

The distinction between grief and a recognised psychiatric condition was again discussed in *Vernon v Bosley (No 1)* [1997]. The claimant was found to suffer from post-traumatic stress disorder (PTSD), complicated by a grief reaction. While PTSD is recoverable because it is a recognised psychiatric condition, grief is not compensatable. It was held by a majority that, although the rules of nervous shock limit the number of potential claimants, they do not limit the compensation to those who are owed a duty of care. Even though part of the injury was attributable to grief, damages were recoverable in full.

Additional criteria
In addition to the above, there are other criteria that a secondary victim will have to satisfy before they can recover for nervous shock:

■ proximity in terms of relationship – the claimant must have close ties of love and affection with the accident victim. Rescuers are an exception to this rule;

■ proximity in terms of time and space – the claimant must be at the scene of the accident, in the vicinity of the accident or come across the 'immediate aftermath' of the accident;

■ reasonable foreseeability – the claimant's injuries must have been reasonably foreseeable;

■ there must have been a direct perception of the accident by the claimant with his own 'unaided senses'.

Proximity in terms of relationship
Own safety. Initially, the law allowed recovery only where the claimant had been put in fear of his own safety, see *Dulieu v White* [1901]. The claimant in

McFarlane v EE Caledonia Ltd [1994] was a rescuer at the Piper Alpha disaster. It was held that he could not recover damages even though he was not a person of reasonable fortitude, as he had feared for his own safety.

Fear for the safety of others. Eventually, the law was extended so that recovery was allowed where the claimant feared for the safety of others. *Hambrook v Stokes* [1925] is authority for this proposition, although it should be noted that this is a difficult case and evidence was adduced that the claimant had feared for her own safety.

Close and loving relationship. In *Alcock v Chief Constable of South Yorkshire* [1991], it was held by the House of Lords that the claimant had to be in a 'close and loving relationship' with the accident victim. This approach rejected an earlier approach by the Court of Appeal, which tried to put a restriction on the amount of claims by limiting claimants to specific categories, such as parents and spouses.

Nervous shock caused through damage to property. The cases looked at so far have concentrated on nervous shock following the negligent infliction of personal injury on a loved one. Claims have been allowed for damage to property as well as physical injury. The Court of Appeal in *Attia v British Gas* [1987] allowed for nervous shock after the claimant witnessed her house burning down as a result of the defendant's negligence in installing central heating.

Rescuers and employees. As explained above, in *Frost v Chief Constable of South Yorkshire* [1999] the House of Lords held that rescuers and employees who were not within the zone of physical danger were secondary victims, and must therefore satisfy the 'close and loving relationship' test.

However, rescuers who are employees may be successful in claims for psychiatric injury if the employer fails to provide counselling after the traumatic event. In *Leach v Chief Constable of Gloucestershire*, the Court of Appeal held that there was no duty of care owed to a voluntary worker who had acted as an 'appropriate adult' during police interviews with Fred West, a notorious serial killer. Nevertheless, the case did proceed on the issue of failure to provide counselling afterwards.

Proximity in terms of time and space

Initially, the claimant had to be at the scene of the accident to be able to recover for nervous shock. In *Bourhill v Young* [1942], the claimant was 50 yards from the scene of the accident which she could hear but could not see and was held to be insufficiently proximate to the scene of the accident. Similarly, in *King v Phillips* [1953], the defendant was a taxi driver who negligently ran over a boy's tricycle. The claimant was the boy's mother who witnessed the accident from a distance of 70 yards. It was held that she was insufficiently proximate to the scene of the accident.

However, a change can be detected in the courts' attitude in *Boardman v Sanderson* [1964], where the claimant, who again heard but was not present at the scene of the accident, was able to recover.

In *McLoughlin v O'Brian* [1982], the claimant was two miles from the accident, but rushed to the hospital to see her family prior to them receiving medical treatment and was held to be sufficiently proximate. She had come across the 'immediate aftermath' of the accident. On the other hand, in *Palmer v Tees Health Authority* [1999], the claim of a mother who saw the body of her murdered child three days after death failed for lack of proximity.

In *Duncan v British Coal Corp* [1997], a claimant who was 275 metres away from the scene of the accident and arrived at the scene four minutes later, but saw no injury or blood, was not sufficiently proximate in terms of time and space.

Reasonable foreseeability

In *Bourhill v Young*, the claimant did not recover as she was not regarded as being reasonably foreseeable. Two views formed as to the true *ratio* of the case:

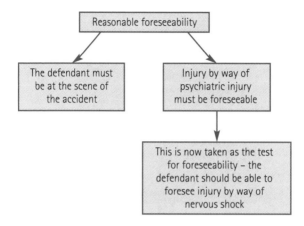

Direct perception

In *McLoughlin v O'Brian* [1982], certain policy issues came to the fore. Lord Wilberforce felt that there was a need to set some limit on the extent of liability and it was therefore necessary to limit claims where there had been a direct perception of the accident with the claimant's own unaided senses. Lord Bridge did not see the necessity of setting such an arbitrary limit on claims.

For several years after *McLoughlin v O'Brian*, there was considerable uncertainty as to the state of the law. In *Hevican v Ruane* [1991], the claimant saw his son's dead body some time after he died, without coming across the 'immediate aftermath' of the accident. Similarly, at first instance, in *Ravenscroft v Rederiaktiebølaget Transatlantic* [1992], the claim of a mother who did not come across the 'immediate aftermath' was initially allowed.

Alcock v Chief Constable of South Yorkshire [1991] settled the fact that it had to be a direct perception of the accident with the claimant's own unaided senses. *Ravenscroft v Rederiaktiebølaget Transatlantic* was, as a result, overturned on appeal.

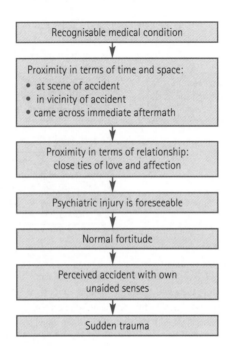

PROPOSALS FOR REFORM

The Law Commission in its 1998 report, *Liability for Psychiatric Illness*, recommended reform. It felt that there should be a statutory 'duty of care'. It would leave the rule in *Page v Smith* unaffected but would otherwise require reasonable foreseeability of psychiatric illness as a result of death, injury or imperilment of a person with whom the claimant had a close tie of love and affection, regardless of proximity in terms of time and space. Furthermore, the claimant would no longer be required to perceive the accident with his own unaided senses.

When proving proximity in terms of love and affection, there would be a fixed set of relationships covered by the statutory duty of care. This would include the following categories of relationship:

▓ spouse;

- parent;

- child;

- brother or sister (but not step brothers and sisters);

- cohabitees of at least two years' standing (including same sex relationships).

Anyone not included in the list would have to prove close ties of love and affection. The statutory duty would not be imposed if it was not 'just and reasonable' to do so. This is in line with the *Caparo* test.

ECONOMIC LOSS

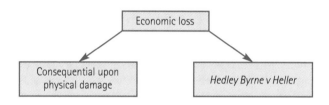

The law of negligence does not give the same level of protection to economic interests as it does to physical interests. There are only three types of situation where recovery is allowed in negligence for economic loss:

- economic loss which is consequential upon physical damage;

- negligent misstatements;

- 'pockets' of liability which are thought to survive, see *Murphy v Brentwood DC* [1990].

ECONOMIC LOSS CONSEQUENTIAL UPON PHYSICAL DAMAGE

It is long established that economic loss as a result of physical injury is recoverable not only for the cost of repairing physical damage to person or property but also for 'consequential' loss of earnings or profits during convalescence or repair.

Much stricter controls apply in relation to 'commercial losses'. Recovery was not allowed in *Weller & Co v Foot and Mouth Disease Research Institute* [1965], even though the damage was foreseeable, as damage was also foreseeable to 'countless other enterprises'.

In *Spartan Steel and Alloys v Martin & Co (Contractors) Ltd* [1972], the defendant negligently cut off electricity to the claimant's factory. Damages for the cost of molten metal which was thrown away were recoverable, as the loss was consequential upon physical damage, but loss of profits while the electricity was cut off were not recoverable as they were purely commercial profits.

This area was greatly affected by the application of the *Anns* test. In *Junior Books v Veitchi Co Ltd* [1982], recovery was allowed for economic loss in a situation where liability had not been held to exist before. The defendants were subcontractors and flooring specialists and had been nominated by the clamaints who had employed the main contractors. The floor was negligently laid and the claimants claimed loss of profits for the period when the floor had to be re-laid. Applying the *Anns* test, it was held that the damage was recoverable. This promised to open up a whole new field of claims for economic loss and *Junior Books* has not been followed in subsequent cases, although it has not been formally overruled. The House of Lords found it particularly significant that the subcontractors had been nominated by the clamaints, and it was felt that this was sufficient to create a relationship of 'proximity'.

This has become known as the 'high water' mark of economic loss. The courts have since returned to the traditional test. For example, in *Muirhead v Industrial Tank Specialities Ltd* [1985], the claimants, who had suffered loss because their lobsters had been killed as a result of defective motors on a tank, could only recover the cost of the lobsters and repairs to the tank; they could not recover for loss of profits. This case has clear echoes of *Spartan Steel*.

This trend was confirmed by the case of *Leigh and Sillavan v Aliakmon Shipping* [1986], which again held that it was not possible to recover economic losses arising from negligent misconduct.

NEGLIGENT MISSTATEMENTS
So far we have looked at liability for negligent acts; the situation is very different when it comes to statements which cause economic loss. One difficulty is that

statements may be made on an informal occasion and may be passed on without the consent of the speaker.

Special relationship

The major development in this area came in the case of *Hedley Byrne & Co Ltd v Heller & Partners* [1963], where the House of Lords held that where there was a 'special relationship' between the maker of a statement and the receiver of that statement then there could be liability for the economic loss caused. In this particular case, there was no liability as there had been a disclaimer attached to the statement, so there had not been a 'voluntary assumption of responsibility'.

The Privy Council in *Mutual Life and Citizens' Assurance Co Ltd v Evatt* [1971] attempted to limit the scope of *Hedley Byrne* by stating that it applied only in respect of advice given in the course of a business and where the defendant made it clear that he was claiming some special skill or competence. (There was, however, a minority view rejecting this approach.)

That attempt has not been followed since and the special relationship has been drawn more liberally. It became clear in *Howard Marine and Dredging Co Ltd v Ogden* [1978] that there had to be *considered* advice which someone would act upon. Liability would not extend to off-the-cuff information.

So, in *Esso Petroleum v Mardon* [1976], the defendants were liable even though they were not in the business of giving advice; they *did* have experience and special skill and knowledge compared to the claimants.

While in *Henderson v Merrett Syndicates Ltd* [1994] there was liability for advice given under a contract, in *Holt v Payne Skillington* [1995] it was held that the duty under *Hedley Byrne* could be greater than that in contract.

The Privy Council, in *Royal Bank Trust Co Ltd (Trinidad) Ltd v Pampellonne* [1987], made a distinction between passing on information and the giving of advice. See also *Williams v Natural Life Health Foods* [1998] (HL).

In *Chaudhry v Prabhakar* [1988], liability was imposed when the statement was made on a social occasion but the defendant had specialist knowledge compared to the claimant.

RELIANCE

There must be reliance on the statement by the claimant. Take, for example, *Smith v Eric S Bush* [1989] and *Harris v Wyre Forest DC* [1990], two appeals heard together by the House of Lords.

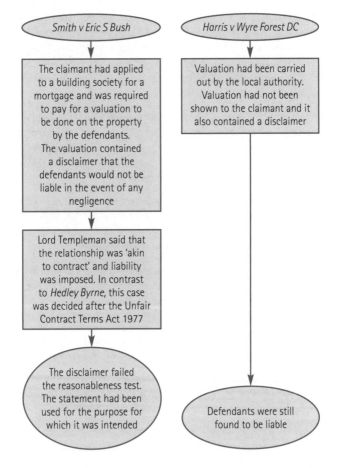

Smith v Eric S Bush

The claimant had applied to a building society for a mortgage and was required to pay for a valuation to be done on the property by the defendants.
The valuation contained a disclaimer that the defendants would not be liable in the event of any negligence

Lord Templeman said that the relationship was 'akin to contract' and liability was imposed. In contrast to *Hedley Byrne*, this case was decided after the Unfair Contract Terms Act 1977

The disclaimer failed the reasonableness test. The statement had been used for the purpose for which it was intended

Harris v Wyre Forest DC

Valuation had been carried out by the local authority. Valuation had not been shown to the claimant and it also contained a disclaimer

Defendants were still found to be liable

By contrast, a firm of estate agents could rely on a disclaimer in property particulars as against the purchaser of a property in *McCullagh v Lane Fox and*

Partners Ltd [1995]. The purchaser had not, in that case, been reasonably entitled to believe that the estate agent, at the time of making the statement, was assuming responsibility for it. The inclusion of a disclaimer put the matter beyond doubt. The Unfair Contract Terms Act 1977 did not preclude the estate agent from relying on the disclaimer.

It was held in *Hemmens v Wilson Browne* [1993] that it could not be reasonable to rely on a statement where a solicitor had advised his client's mistress to obtain independent legal advice before executing a document.

In addition to reliance, there must be knowledge by the maker of the statement that the recipient will rely on the statement to his detriment. Both requirements were satisfied in *Welton v North Cornwall District Council* [1996]. An environmental health officer negligently required the owner of food premises to comply with the Food Act 1990, by making unnecessary substantial building works and major alterations to the kitchen. He also threatened to close the business down if the works were not completed. The officer knew that what he said would be relied on by the claimant without independent inquiry. He visited to inspect and approved the works. The fact that the relationship arose out of the purported exercise of statutory functions did not give rise to an immunity on the part of the local authority. It was not necessary to consider whether it was fair, just and reasonable to impose a duty, as the case did not involve an incremental extension to the *Hedley Byrne* principle.

PURPOSE

The courts will take into account the purpose for which the statement was made. In *Caparo Industries plc v Dickman* [1990], the claimants were shareholders in a company and, as such, were entitled to annual audited accounts. On the basis of these accounts, they launched a takeover bid in the company before discovering that the accounts had been negligently audited and had wrongly shown the company to be profit-making. The claimants sued the auditors, who were found not to be liable. The annual audited accounts were the fulfilment of a statutory obligation, the purpose of which was to enable the shareholders to take decisions about the management of the company; they were not intended to be the basis of an investment decision.

27

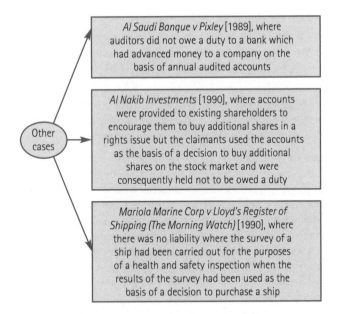

Al Saudi Banque v Pixley [1989], where auditors did not owe a duty to a bank which had advanced money to a company on the basis of annual audited accounts

Al Nakib Investments [1990], where accounts were provided to existing shareholders to encourage them to buy additional shares in a rights issue but the claimants used the accounts as the basis of a decision to buy additional shares on the stock market and were consequently held not to be owed a duty

Mariola Marine Corp v Lloyd's Register of Shipping (The Morning Watch) [1990], where there was no liability where the survey of a ship had been carried out for the purposes of a health and safety inspection when the results of the survey had been used as the basis of a decision to purchase a ship

Other cases

NEGLIGENT STATEMENTS RELIED UPON BY A THIRD PARTY

An employer who gives a negligent reference about an employee to a prospective employer owes a duty not only to the prospective employer but also to the employee. In *Spring v Guardian Assurance plc* [1994], it was held by the House of Lords that there could be liability in negligence to an employee for an inaccurate reference under the *Hedley Byrne* principle.

This overturned the decision of the Court of Appeal in the same case which held that any right of action would be in defamation where there would be the defence of qualified privilege. This defence would be defeated by the claimant only if malice could be proved, which is extremely difficult.

Similar situations have arisen where a doctor has examined a claimant on behalf of someone else, such as a company. In *Baker v Kaye* [1997], a doctor carried out a preemployment medical assessment on behalf of a company. It was held that, in such circumstances, a doctor could owe a duty of care to the prospective employee, although, on the facts of the case, there had been no breach of duty. The case was distinguished from *Spring* as there had never been a contractual relationship between the prospective employer and employee, but it was regarded as just and reasonable to impose a duty.

In *Kapfunde v Abbey National plc* [1998], the claimant applied for a job and filled in a medical questionnaire. A doctor who considered the questionnaire felt that the claimant might be frequently absent from work. The Court of Appeal held that there was no duty of care owed by the doctor to the claimant as there was insufficient proximity. The Court of Appeal disapproved of the decision in *Baker v Kaye*.

VOLUNTARY ASSUMPTION OF RESPONSIBILITY OTHER THAN FOR NEGLIGENT MISSTATEMENTS

There is a line of cases that allows recovery for pure economic loss in negligence when the special skills of a provider of professional services has been relied on by someone other than his client.

In *Ross v Caunters* [1979], a solicitor allowed the spouse of a beneficiary to witness a will. As a result, the gift to the beneficiary lapsed. It was held that the solicitor was liable to the beneficiary, as damage to her could have been foreseen and she belonged to a closed category of persons.

Ross v Caunters was decided during the period of the *Anns* test. It was uncertain after the demise of that test whether this type of economic loss would remain recoverable. It was found to have survived in the House of Lords decision of *White v Jones* [1995]. The testator of a will cut his two daughters out of his estate following a quarrel. After a reconciliation with his daughters, he sent a letter instructing a firm of solicitors that legacies of £9,000 should be given to each of his two daughters, the claimants. The letter was received on 17 July and nothing was done by the solicitors for a month. On 16 August, the firm's managing clerk asked the firm's probate department to draw up a will or codicil incorporating the new legacies. The following day the managing clerk went on holiday. On his return, a fortnight later, he arranged to see the testator on 17 September. The testator died on 14 September before the new will had been executed.

Lord Goff held that the claimants were owed a duty of care as otherwise there would be a lacuna in the law. The solicitor owes a duty of care to his client and generally owes no duty to a third party. If an extension to the *Hedley Byrne* principle were not allowed, there would be no method of enforcing the contractual right. Those who had a valid claim (the testator and his estate) had suffered no loss. Those who had suffered a loss (the disappointed beneficiaries) would not have a valid claim. Lord Browne-Wilkinson found that the situation was analogous to *Hedley Byrne*.

It was held in *Hemmens v Wilson Browne* [1993] that the principle would not extend to an *inter vivos* transaction (that is, one made while the testator is still alive), as it would always be possible to rectify a mistake.

White v Jones could not be relied on in *Goodwill v British Pregnancy Advisory Service* [1996]. A woman who knew that her partner had undergone a vasectomy did not use any form of contraception and subsequently became pregnant. Her partner had been assured by the defendants that the operation had been successful and that future contraception was unnecessary. It was argued that the situation was analogous to *White v Jones*. The claimant was not owed a duty as it was not known that the advice would be communicated to the advisee and would be acted upon by her. She belonged to an indeterminate class of women with whom the man could have formed a relationship after the operation.

Some indication of the scope of the duty is provided by *Woodward v Wolferstans* [1997]. The claimant had purchased a property, raising 95 per cent of the purchase price by way of mortgage. The defendants were a firm of solicitors who acted for her father who guaranteed the mortgage. There was no contact between the firm and the claimant. After the mortgage fell into arrears, the lender commenced possession proceedings. It was held that the defendants had assumed responsibility for tasks which were known or ought to be known to closely affect the claimant's economic wellbeing. This did not extend to explaining the details of the transaction and the implications of the mortgage.

In *Carr-Glynn v Frearsons* [1998], the solicitor had negligently failed to sever a joint tenancy held by the deceased, with the result that when she died, her right in the land was extinguished. Thus, the testatrix and her estate *had* suffered a loss (cf *White v Jones*, above). Lloyd J held that this excluded an action by the intended beneficiaries under the will, but the Court of Appeal allowed the appeal, saying that *White v Jones* allowed them to extend the duty to this new situation (although it was emphasised that the estate and the beneficiaries could not both sue the solicitor with respect to the same loss).

A BROADER PRINCIPLE?

In *HM Customs & Excise Commissioners v Barclays Bank* [2006], the defendant bank was served with a freezing injunction, instructing it not to allow one of its clients to remove any assets from his account. The bank failed to comply with this order, meaning that the client, with whom customs were engaged in litigation, had no assets to satisfy judgment against him in their favour. Customs sued the bank for this loss, in negligence. The bank argued that this being a case of pure economic loss, it could be liable only in the exceptional event of a voluntary assumption of responsibility to the claimant. There was no such assumption because the bank had not undertaken anything of its own volition – rather, it had been ordered to take the relevant action by the court order. The bank simply had no choice. While this argument succeeded at trial, the Court of Appeal held that the bank did owe a duty of care to customs. The absence of voluntary assumption of responsibility was not fatal. The bank was anyway under a duty not to allow the assets to be withdrawn, and there was no reason why this duty should not extend to customs in tort, since they had suffered loss as a result of the bank's failure. The Court of Appeal decision was overturned by the House of Lords. The bank owed no duty of care to the claimants. The injunction was only enforceable by the court. The documentation issued by the court did not hint at the existence of any other remedy. That regime made perfect sense on the assumption that the only duty owed by a notified party was to the court. It could not be suggested that the customer owed a duty to the party which obtained an order, since they were opposing parties in litigation and no duty was owed by a litigating party to its opponent. A duty of care in tort might co-exist with a similar duty in contract or a statutory duty and in principle a tortious duty of care owed to the claimants could co-exist with a duty of compliance owed to the court. There was, however, no instance in which a non-consensual court order, without more, had been held to give rise to a duty of care owed to the party obtaining the order. The question whether in all the circumstances it was fair, just and reasonable to impose a duty of care on the defendant towards the claimant was determinative. In the instant case it was unjust and unreasonable that the bank should, on being notified of an order which it had no opportunity to resist, become exposed to a liability which was in the instant case for a few million pounds only, but might in another case be very much more.

In particular, what is the proper approach to novel claims for pure economic loss if 'assumption of responsibility' is not the key question (as we were told by the House of Lords in *Henderson v Merrett Syndicates Ltd* [1994])?

LIABILITY OF PUBLIC AUTHORITIES

This area deals with the question of whether public authorities exercising statutory powers owe any duty to a private individual suffering loss or injury resulting from the authority's negligence.

There are three problems in this area:

▓ many statutory powers confer a discretion as to how and whether the relevant power should be exercised;

▓ where the alleged negligence is a failure to exercise statutory power, the question of liability for omissions is raised in its most obvious form;

▓ recent case law requires the individual to pursue a remedy in the form of judicial review as opposed to tort.

The problem of whether a duty of care will ever be imposed in respect of the negligent exercise of statutory powers and the problem of liability for failure to exercise a power can now be considered together.

In *Home Office v Dorset Yacht Co Ltd* [1970], the Home Office had a wide discretion as to how to run its Borstal Training Schools. If the Home Office owed a duty to individuals for damage caused by escaping trainees, then it might be inhibited in the exercise of its discretion. Lord Diplock stipulated that the Home Office would be liable only for *ultra vires* acts of its servants. The borstal officers had disregarded an order and so their conduct was *ultra vires*. The duty was owed only to those in the immediate vicinity whose property was foreseeably likely to be damaged or stolen by escaping inmates.

This reasoning was further developed in *Anns v Merton LBC* [1977], where the local authority argued that it had merely exercised a power and had not been under a mandatory duty to inspect the foundations of all new buildings. The authority argued that:

- it would not be liable for omitting to inspect; and

- if it was not liable for inspecting, it could not be liable for negligent inspection.

Again, it was stated that *ultra vires* conduct could create a duty of care, and that *ultra vires* conduct could include a failure to exercise a power at all, or an improper exercise of that power.

The House of Lords made a distinction between:

- planning/policy decisions; and

- operational decisions,

and stated that it would be far more likely to find a duty of care where there had been an operational error and would be less likely to interfere with policy matters.

Although *Anns* was overruled by *Murphy v Brentwood DC*, the policy/ operational dichotomy is still valid. It was said in *Rowling v Takaro* [1988] that there was no automatic liability for operational decisions but the distinction could be seen as a preliminary filter. Policy decisions would be automatically filtered out, but once this step had been overcome then there was a need to decide whether a duty should be imposed on the basis of foreseeability, proximity and whether it was fair, just and reasonable to do so.

There has been a trend of restricting the tort of negligence in this area. In *Yuen Kun-Yeu v AG of Hong Kong* [1987], *Rowling v Takaro Properties* [1988] and *Davis v Radcliffe* [1990], the factors that were cited as militating against a duty of care were similar. For example, the distorting effect of potential liability on the decision-making process; the waste of public money involved in civil servants cautiously investigating the case to the detriment of other members of the public; the difficulty of ever proving negligence in the making of such a decision; and the difficulty of distinguishing the cases in which legal advice should have been sought.

This generally restrictive approach to negligence claims in this area appears to be due to a reluctance to introduce the tortious duty of care where there is an existing system of redress or the statutory regulatory system has made no provision for individual claims.

This trend towards the containment of negligence claims can be seen in *Jones v Department of Employment* [1988], where one of the grounds of the Court of Appeal's decision that a social security adjudication officer owed no duty of care to a claimant was that the duty of the adjudication officer lay in the sphere of public law and was enforceable only by way of statutory appeals procedure or by judicial review.

The House of Lords again held that policy decisions were outside the scope of negligence in *X v Bedfordshire County Council* [1995]. It was held that where a statutory discretion was imposed on a local authority, it was for the authority to exercise the discretion and nothing that the authority might do within the ambit of the discretion could be actionable at common law.

Where the decision complained of fell outside the statutory discretion, it could give rise to common law liability, but where the factors relevant to the exercise of the discretion included matters of policy, the court could not adjudicate on such policy matters and therefore could not reach the decision that it was outside the statutory ambit.

The same conclusion was reached in *Stovin v Wise* [1996]. A highway authority was held not to be liable in negligence for failing to remove a hazard to the highway under statutory powers conferred by the Highway Act 1980, even though the authority was aware of the danger and had decided that it ought to remove the hazard but had failed to do so.

Lord Hoffmann said that the minimum preconditions for basing a duty of care on the existence of a statutory power were, first, that it would have to have been irrational not to have exercised the power, so that there was a public duty to act and, secondly, that there were exceptional grounds for holding that the policy of the statute required compensation to be paid to persons who suffered loss because the power was not exercised.

Stovin v Wise was distinguished by the Court of Appeal in *Kane v New Forest District Council* [2001]. It was held that the council might owe a duty to prevent developers opening to the public a dangerous footpath, when the council itself had required a footpath to be included as part of the housing development.

Another reason advanced for not imposing a duty on public authorities is that it would lead to defensiveness in their decision making. In *Harris v Evans* [1998], a health and safety inspector making negligently excessive requirements of bungee jump operators when making recommendations as to whether activities should be authorised under the Health and Safety at Work etc Act 1974, was held not liable. It was an inevitable part of the system of regulation that it would have adverse impacts for certain sections of society. There was an appeals mechanism built into the legislation, and a common law duty of care would lead to inspectors being defensive in the exercise of their enforcement powers under the Act.

The recent case law in this area has not been entirely consistent. Some decisions of the House of Lords have been more generous to claimants. In *Barrett v Enfield LBC* [1999] it was held that a local authority arguably owed a duty to properly bring up a child whom it had taken into care at a young age. In *Phelps v Hillingdon LBC* [2000] a local authority was held liable when its educational psychologists failed to diagnose the claimants' dyslexia, with the result that they were not classified as having special educational needs. In *JD v East Berkshire NHS Trust* [2005], the House held that an authority investigating (unfounded) allegations of child abuse did not owe a duty to the parents involved, because this might interfere with the fearless discharge of the primary duty to the children. However, their Lordships stated that *X v Bedfordshire* was no longer good law, having been overtaken by cases such as *Barrett* and *Phelps*, as well as the enactment of the Human Rights Act 1998. Thus, it is likely that a duty would now be owed to children in this situation.

A decision going against this trend is *Gorringe v Calderdale MBC* [2004]. The claimant crashed her car, and sued the highway authority for failing to paint 'SLOW' on the road. It was held that there was no breach of the statutory duty to maintain the highway. Moreover, the statutory duty to promote road safety did not give rise to a claim in damages at the suit of an injured individual. In such a situation, the House of Lords held, the *statutory* duties (unenforceable as such) could not conjure up a *common law* duty of care where none would otherwise exist. The case confirms that public authorities are not normally liable for pure omissions. In this it seems reminiscent of *Stovin v Wise* (above), although *Gorringe* is a stronger case since it was put on the basis of breach of statutory *duty*, rather than failure to exercise a statutory *power*.

BREACH OF DUTY: STANDARD OF CARE

The second element in negligence is whether the defendant has breached the duty of care. The defendant will have fulfilled his duty if he has behaved in accordance with the standard of the reasonable man. This is an objective standard and disregards the personal idiosyncrasies of the defendant.

The question of whether a person has fulfilled a particular duty is a question of *fact*. It was held by the House of Lords in *Qualcast (Wolverhampton) Ltd v Haynes* [1959] that reasonableness will depend on the circumstances of the case and it is a mistake to rely on previous cases as precedents for what constitutes negligence. So, in *Worsfold v Howe* [1980], the trial judge held that a driver who had edged out from a side road and across stationary tankers before colliding with a motorcyclist was negligent, as the Court of Appeal had ruled that similar actions were negligent in a previous case. The Court of Appeal, though, held that the previous case laid down no legal principle, and that such decisions were to be treated as questions of fact.

FACTORS OF THE OBJECTIVE STANDARD
The law provides various guiding principles as to the objective standard.

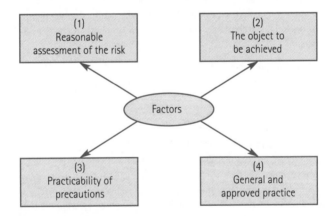

(1) Reasonable assessment of the risk
This can be further subdivided into two factors:

- degree of likelihood of harm occurring; and

- seriousness of the harm that may occur.

(a) *Degree of likelihood of harm occurring.* A reasonable man is not usually expected to take precautions against something where there is only a small risk of it occurring. Two cricketing cases provide a simple illustration:

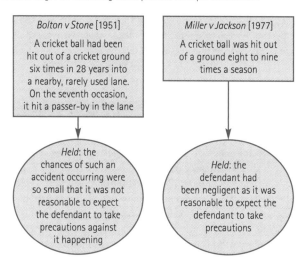

Difference: the crucial difference between the two cases is that the risk of harm was much greater in *Miller v Jackson* than in *Bolton v Stone*.

(b) *Seriousness of the harm that may occur.* This is an exception to the above; that is, where there is a small risk but the potential harm that may occur is great, then a reasonable man would be expected to take precautions.

> ▶ **PARIS v STEPNEY BC [1951]**
>
> The claimant was blind in one eye. While he was working for the defendants, a metal chip entered his good eye and rendered him totally blind. The defendants were found to be negligent in failing to supply him with goggles as, even though there had only been a small risk, the consequences were serious.

(2) The object to be achieved

The importance of the object to be attained is also a factor which is taken into account when deciding the standard of care. It is necessary to assess the utility of the defendant's act. The greater its social utility, the greater the likelihood of the defendant's behaviour being assessed as reasonable.

In *Cole v Davis-Gilbert* [2007] the social utility of traditional English village green community activities such as fêtes and maypole dancing were considered by the Court of Appeal. It was said that if the law courts were to set a higher standard of care than what is reasonable, the consequences would be quickly felt and that such activities would not take place for fear of what might go wrong.

▶ WATT v HERTFORDSHIRE CC [1954]

The claimant was a fireman and part of a rescue team that was rushing to the scene of an accident to rescue a woman trapped under a car. The claimant was injured by a heavy piece of equipment which had not been properly secured on the lorry on which it was travelling in the emergency circumstances. It was held that it was necessary to 'balance the risk against the object to be achieved'. The action for negligence failed as the risk of the equipment causing injury in transit was not so great as to prevent the efforts to save the woman's life.

▶ LATIMER v AEC LTD [1953]

The defendant's factory was flooded; the water mixed with factory oil and made the floor slippery. Sawdust was spread on the surface, but not enough to cover the whole affected area. The employers were held not to be negligent.

(3) Practicability of precautions

The cost of avoiding a risk is also a material factor in the standard of care. The defendant will not be expected to spend vast sums of money on avoiding a risk which is very small.

In *Latimer* it was held that the employers were not negligent. It was necessary to balance the risk against the measures necessary to eliminate it. In this case the risk was not so great as to justify the expense of closing the factory down.

(4) General and approved practice

If it is shown that the defendant acted in accordance with general and approved practice then this may be strong evidence that he has not been negligent. However, this is not conclusive, and a defendant may still be negligent even though he acted in accordance with a common practice.

There is an obligation on the defendant to keep up to date with developments and to change practices in the light of new knowledge: *Stokes v Guest, Keen and Nettlefold (Bolts and Nuts) Ltd* [1968].

It will not be a defence to say that general and approved practice has been followed if it is an obvious folly to do so. 'Neglect of duty does not by repetition cease to be neglect of duty,' per Slesser LJ, *Carpenters' Co v British Mutual Banking Co Ltd* [1937].

The doctrine of 'obvious folly' was first expounded by Lord Dunedin in *Morton v William Dixon Ltd* [1909] and an illustration can be found in *Re Herald of Free Enterprise* [1987]. Following the Zeebrugge ferry disaster, the master of the ship claimed that it was general and approved practice for him not to check that the bow doors were closed prior to setting out to sea. It was held that the general and approved practice constituted an 'obvious folly' and should not have been followed.

Failure to comply with a guide to professional conduct is not conclusive proof of negligence (*Johnson v Bingley* [1995]).

When considering the standard of care to be imposed on a parent who was supervising children on a bouncy castle at a children's birthday party, the Court of Appeal had regard to the guidance provided by the hire company (*Harris v Perry* [2008]). It ruled that the first instance decision had imposed too high a standard of care on the parent by requiring uninterrupted supervision as the hire company documents stipulated sufficient supervision to stop, rather than prevent, boisterous behaviour. A further case that concerned that standard of care required when supervising children is *Palmer v Cornwall Country Council* [2009] in which it was held that one person was not adequate to supervise 300 children.

THE GENERAL STANDARD AND SKILLED DEFENDANTS

▶ BOLAM v FRIERN HOSPITAL MANAGEMENT COMMITTEE [1957]

Basic facts

The claimant suffered a broken pelvis whilst undergoing electro-convulsive therapy (ECT). The question for the court was whether the doctor performing the ECT was negligent in failing to give a muscle relaxant to the claimant before treatment began or restraining him during it. Evidence was given of the practices of a number of doctors administering ECT, some who favoured the use of muscle relaxant and others who did not. The action failed.

Relevance

A defendant is not negligent if he acts in accordance with a practice accepted at the time as proper by a responsible body of professional opinion skilled in the particular form of treatment.

Skilled defendants are judged by higher standards than the ordinary defendant. The test for skilled defendants was encapsulated by McNair J in *Bolam*:

> The test is the standard of the ordinary skilled man exercising and professing to have that particular skill.

> A man need not possess the highest expert skill at the risk of being found negligent. It is well established law that it is sufficient if he exercises the ordinary skill of an ordinary competent man exercising that particular art.

It can be seen that skilled defendants must meet a higher standard than the ordinary person, and this is an exception to the rule that everyone is judged by the same standard.

Skilled defendants face a particular problem when trying to invoke the defence of general and approved practice, as often there are conflicting views within a profession as to which course of action is the appropriate course to take. *Bolam* gave an answer to this problem as it stated that a doctor was not negligent if he acted in accordance with a respectable body of opinion merely because another body of opinion took a contrary view. It was also held that a doctor could not be criticised if he believed dangers of treatment were minimal and did not stress them to the patient.

Bolam was applied in the case of *Sidaway v Bethlem Royal Hospital Govrs* [1985], where it was held that a doctor was under a duty to inform a patient of special/real risks, but this is subject to an overriding duty to act in the patient's best interest.

However, conditions were attached to the *Bolam* test in *Bolitho v City and Hackney Health Authority* [1997]. A two-year-old boy suffered brain damage as a result of bronchial air passages becoming blocked leading to cardiac arrest. It was agreed that the only course of action to prevent the damage was to have the boy intubated. The doctor who negligently failed to attend the boy said that she would not have intubated had she attended. There was evidence from one expert witness that he would not have intubated, whereas five other experts said that they would have done so.

The House of Lords held that there would have to be a logical basis for the opinion not to intubate. This would involve a weighing of risks against benefit in order to achieve a defensible conclusion. In effect, this means that a judge will be entitled to choose between two bodies of expert opinion and to reject an opinion which is 'logically indefensible'.

Trainee experts

The potential harshness of the objective standard for skilled defendants is illustrated by the case of *Wilsher v Essex Area Health Authority* [1988], when it was stated that a young, inexperienced doctor is judged by the standards of a competent experienced doctor even though he has not yet reached that standard.

Experts outside the medical field

The same principles extend outside the medical sphere. In *Wells v Cooper* [1958], the Court of Appeal held that a householder performing a DIY task was judged by the standard of a reasonably competent carpenter.

In *Philips v William Whiteley* [1938], the court rejected the idea that a jeweller who carried out an ear-piercing operation should be judged by the standard of a surgeon; instead the court said that she should be judged by the standard of a reasonably competent jeweller carrying out that particular task.

In *Nettleship v Weston* [1971], a learner driver was judged by the standard of a 'competent and experienced driver' as she held herself out as possessing a certain standard of skill and experience. The court felt that a uniform standard of skill was preferable because of the practical difficulty of assessing a particular person's actual skill or experience.

Expert standard depends on the surrounding circumstances
Like the ordinary standard, the expert standard depends on the circumstances of the particular case.

In *Wooldridge v Sumner* [1962], a momentary lapse on the part of a show-jumper did not make him negligent, even though he injured a spectator.

In *Smoldon v Whitworth* [1996], the court held that a rugby referee's level of care to a participant in a sporting event was appropriate in all the circumstances. The threshold of liability was a high one and would not be easily crossed. On the facts of the case, the referee was liable for spinal injuries caused by a collapsed scrum.

ABNORMAL DEFENDANTS
Further exceptions to the rule that everyone is judged by the same standard in assessing whether they are negligent are children, the insane and the physically ill. These categories are treated separately and different principles apply.

(1) Children
In *Gough v Thorne* [1966], Lord Denning MR said that a 12-year-old child could not be contributorily negligent. In *Walmsley v Humenick* [1954], it was held that very young children were incapable of negligence as they were incapable of foreseeing harm. It should be noted that in tort there is no fixed age for liability, unlike in criminal law.

A problem with children has been in deciding whether subjective circumstances, such as the child's mental ability and maturity, should be taken into account or whether an objective standard should be applied in the same way as foradults.

The High Court of Australia in *McHale v Watson* [1966] held that a 12-year-old boy should be judged by 'the foresight and prudence of an ordinary boy of 12'.

McHale v Watson was followed by the Court of Appeal in *Mullin v Richards* [1998]. Two 15-year-old girls were playing with plastic rulers when one broke and a piece of plastic entered the claimant's eye. The test was whether the risk of injury would have been foreseeable to an ordinarily prudent and reasonable 15-year-old girl.

(2) The insane and the physically ill

The principles that apply here seem to revolve around whether the defendant was aware of his condition and also whether the defendant had control over his own actions.

Defendant is unaware of the condition

In *Waugh v Allan* [1964], the defendant, a lorry driver, was in the habit of suffering gastric attacks which normally passed quickly. After one such attack, the defendant pulled off the road. When he felt better, he continued on his journey, only to suffer a fatal coronary thrombosis and injure the claimant. The defendant was held not to be negligent as he had recovered sufficient skill and judgment to continue his journey.

In *Jones v Dennison* [1971], the defendant was unaware that he suffered from blackout attacks as a result of epilepsy. He suffered a blackout while driving, injuring the claimant. It was held that he could not be considered negligent, as he was unaware of his tendency to black out.

Defendant retains control over his actions

In situations where the defendant retains some control over his actions, he may be held liable.

In *Morris v Marsden* [1952], the defendant suffered from a mental disease which robbed him of his moral judgment. While suffering from this disease, he attacked and injured the claimant; while he knew the nature and quality of his act, he did not know that what he was doing was wrong. The defendant was held to be liable.

However, in *Mansfield v Weetabix* [1998], a lorry driver crashed when his mental state was impaired by low blood sugar. Even though he had not completely lost consciousness or control (he had attempted to brake at the last minute), he was held not to be liable, as he was unaware of the condition which led to the mental impairment. Leggatt LJ commented that to hold the driver to an objective standard of care which ignored his condition would be strict, and not negligence based, liability.

PROOF OF BREACH

The burden of proof rests with the claimant on the balance of probabilities. However, there may be ways in which the claimant can receive assistance in discharging that burden of proof.

(1) Assistance by statute

Section 11 of the Civil Evidence Act 1968. Where the defendant has been convicted of criminal proceedings, that conviction will be admissible in civil proceedings and the defendant will be presumed to have committed the acts until the contrary is proved.

For example, proof of the defendant's conviction for careless driving places the burden of disproving the occurrence of negligent driving on the defendant.

(2) Assistance at common law

Res ipsa loquitur. 'The thing speaks for itself'. This doctrine originally began with the case of *Scott v London and St Katherine's Dock* [1865]. First, it should be noted that it is an evidential burden and, secondly, three conditions must apply before it can be invoked:

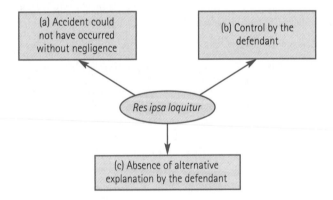

(a) Accident could not have occurred without negligence
For example, stones are not found in buns unless someone has been negligent: *Chapronière v Mason* [1905]; barrels of flour do not fall from warehouse windows onto the street in the absence of negligence: *Byrne v Boadle* [1863]. On the other hand, losses on the commodity market are not *prima facie*

evidence of negligence on the part of brokers: *Stafford v Conti Commodity Services Ltd* [1981]; nor is a spark from a domestic fire: *Sochacki v Sas* [1947].

In *Scott v London and St Katherine's Dock* [1865], it was said that the accident must have happened in 'the ordinary course of things'. As a result, a question arises as to whether the doctrine can apply to matters which are outside the common experience. In *Mahon v Osborne* [1939], a swab had been left inside a patient after an abdominal operation; Scott LJ thought that the doctrine could not apply to surgical operations as they are outside a judge's common experience. Since then, the Court of Appeal has allowed the doctrine to be invoked in cases of medical negligence in *Cassidy v Ministry of Health* [1951]. Nevertheless, it was said by Lord Denning in *Hucks v Cole* [1993] that *res ipsa loquitur* could be invoked against a doctor only in 'extreme' cases. This adds to the claimant's difficulties in cases of medical negligence, which generally are harder to prove than other types of negligence.

(b) Control by the defendant

If the defendant is not in control of the situation which could not have occurred without negligence then the doctrine cannot be invoked.

In *Easson v London and North Eastern Railway Co* [1944], the railway company could not be said to be in control of railway doors on a journey from Edinburgh to London, because of the possibility of interference by a third party.

This can be contrasted with *Gee v Metropolitan Railway Co* [1873], where someone fell through a train door shortly after the train left the station. Here, it could be said to be under the control of the railway company, as there was no opportunity for third party interference.

(c) Absence of alternative explanation by the defendant

The cause of the accident must be unknown, see *Barkway v South Western Transport* [1950].

The effect of the doctrine of *res ipsa loquitur*

The effect of *res ipsa loquitur* depends on the case, but two views have been formed as to its effect:

■ *An evidential burden of proof is cast on the defendant*

   In other words, the defendant is required to provide a reasonable explanation of how the accident could have occurred without negligence on his part. If he does so then the claimant goes back to square one and must prove on the balance of probabilities that the defendant has been negligent. Support for this view can be found in *Colvilles Ltd v Devine* [1969].

■ *The other view is that it reverses the burden of proof*

The defendant must prove on the balance of probabilities that he has not been negligent. Support for this view can be found in *Henderson v Jenkins* [1969] and *Ward v Tesco Stores* [1976]. The Privy Council in *Ng Chun Pui v Lee Chuen Tat* [1988] stated that the burden of proof does not shift to the defendant but remains with the claimant throughout the case. It has also been argued that if *res ipsa loquitur* reverses the burden of proof then paradoxically a claimant who relies on the maxim will be in a better position than a claimant who establishes a *prima facie* case in some other way.

CAUSATION

The claimant has to prove not only that the defendant owes him a duty of care and has breached his duty, but also that the defendant caused the claimant's loss. This is not always as straightforward as it sounds.

'BUT FOR' TEST

The defendant's breach of duty must as a matter of fact be a cause of the damage. As a preliminary test in deciding whether the defendant's breach has caused the claimant's damage, the courts have developed the 'but for' test. In other words, would the claimant not have suffered the damage 'but for' the event brought about by the defendant?

> ▶ BARNETT v CHELSEA & KENSINGTON HOSPITAL
> MANAGEMENT COMMITTEE [1968]
>
> Basic facts
> Three nightwatchmen called into a hospital at the end of a shift, complaining that they had been vomiting after drinking tea. The nurse on duty consulted a doctor by telephone, and he said that the men should go home and consult their doctor in the morning. Later the same day, the claimant's husband died of arsenic poisoning.

The doctor owed the claimant's husband a duty of care. In failing to examine the claimant's husband the doctor had breached his duty of care, but the hospital was held not to be liable as the breach had not *caused* the death. It was found that the claimant's husband would have died even if the doctor had examined him as no effective treatment was available at that stage.

Relevance

Applying the 'but for' test, would the claimant not have suffered the damage 'but for' the event brought about by the defendant? The answer has to be no.

Further examples of the 'but for' test can be found in *Robinson v Post Office* [1974], where a doctor was held not to be liable for failing to administer a test dose of a drug where it would have failed to have revealed the allergy; *McWilliams v Sir William Arrol and Co Ltd* [1962], where employers were found not to be liable for failing to provide a safety belt where it was proved that the employee would not have worn it even if it had been provided; and *The Empire Jamaica* [1956], where liability was limited to 'actual fault' and the only fault that could be attributed to the owners was a failure to apply for a mate's certificate which would have been granted as a formality.

Nature of the 'but for' test

It is vital to keep the following points in mind:

- the test acts as a preliminary filter, that is, it sifts irrelevant causes from relevant causes;

- it has no application where there are several successive causes of an accident.

SEVERAL SUCCESSIVE CAUSES

The 'but for' test will not be of much assistance where the claimant has been affected by two successive acts or events. In this type of situation there has been a sequence of events and every act in the sequence is a relevant cause as far as the claimant's damage is concerned; so the courts have to decide the operative cause.

The courts have not always been consistent in their approach. One method is to establish whether the later event has added to the claimant's damage; if not then the person who caused the original injury will be liable.

In *Performance Cars Ltd v Abraham* [1961], the claimant's Rolls-Royce had been involved in an accident and the damage involved the cost of respraying the car. Two weeks later, before the respray had been carried out, the defendant was involved in an accident with the claimant for which the defendant accepted responsibility. This time, there was damage to the wing and bumper which necessitated a respray of the lower part of the car. The defendant was not liable as he had not contributed any more damage than had occurred after the first accident.

A similar sequence of events took place in *Baker v Willoughby* [1969]. As a result of the defendants' negligence, the claimant suffered an injury to his left leg. Before the trial and while working at a new job, the claimant was the victim of an armed robbery and suffered gunshot wounds to his left leg, which then had to be amputated. The defendants argued that their liability was extinguished by the second incident. In other words, they were liable only from the date of the accident to the date of the bank robbery. The House of Lords rejected this. They held that the claimant was being compensated for his loss of amenity, that is, the loss of a good left leg, the difference between a damaged leg and a sound leg. The fact that the leg was further damaged at some later date did not alter the fact that he had already been deprived of a perfectly good left leg.

In both of these cases there have been two successive incidents and the second incident has not added to the claimant's loss, so the perpetrator of the first incident has remained liable. This can be contrasted with *Jobling v Associated Dairies Ltd* [1981]. The facts were that the defendants negligently caused an injury to the claimant's back. Three years later and before trial, the claimant was diagnosed as suffering from a condition called mylopathy, which was unrelated to the accident. This time it was accepted, in contrast to the other cases, that the second incident extinguished liability. The main differences between these cases have been identified as follows:

- in *Jobling*, the second incident occurred as a result of a natural condition, whereas in *Baker v Willoughby* there was an intervention by a third party;

policy decisions on the part of the court. If the court had accepted that the second incident extinguished liability in *Baker*, this would have left the defendant without compensation after the second incident.

SIMULTANEOUS EVENTS

The pragmatic approach of the courts was again evident in the case of *Fitzgerald v Lane* [1987]. The facts were that the claimant crossed a pelican crossing when the red light was showing. He was hit by the first defendant's car and thrown onto the car's windscreen, then onto the ground; and while the claimant was lying on the ground the second defendant ran over him. It was impossible to determine each defendant's contribution towards the injury. The claimant could have suffered slight injuries from the first defendant and been badly injured by the second, or vice versa. The court held that after taking into account the claimant's contributory negligence, both defendants were equally liable.

Similarly, in *Jenkins v Holt* [1999], it was held that where two drivers collided, and each could have avoided injury if they had seen the other, they were both equally liable. Bad driving by one did not make him entirely responsible, if each could have avoided a collision.

MULTIPLE CAUSES

So far, we have looked at situations where there has been a sequence of events. Slightly different issues arise when there are several possible causes of an injury. There are two strands of case law:

Where breach of duty materially increases the risk of injury, the defendant will be held liable.

In *McGhee v National Coal Board* [1972], the defendants failed to supply adequate washing facilities. Although this could not be proved to have caused the claimant's dermatitis, there was evidence to suggest that it had increased the risk of contracting the disease. This was sufficient to make the defendants liable.

The more recent trend is to state that for the defendant to be liable, the defendant's cause must be the probable cause.

In *Wilsher v Essex Area Health Authority* [1988], the claimant's injury could have resulted from one of six possible causes. One of these causes was the administration of an excess of oxygen in the first 30 hours after the baby's birth, which had been carried out by the doctor. It was held that the claimant had to prove that the excess of oxygen was the probable cause of the injury, not that it had increased the baby's risk of being born blind.

▶ FAIRCHILD v GLENHAVEN FUNERAL SERVICES [2002]

Basic facts

A group of defendants had exposed the claimants to the risk of injury by asbestos, in successive periods of employment, but it could not be shown when the risk had eventuated and, therefore, which employer had actually caused the injury. (It was found that one single fibre of asbestos could potentially have caused all the damage to each claimant.)

Relevance

The House of Lords held that in this 'exceptional' situation, the increased risk could be equated with proof of causation, and thus all the defendants were liable for the injury.

In the course of their speeches the Law Lords disapproved the explanation of *McGhee* given by the House in *Wilsher.*

In *Barker v Corus UK* [2006] the claimant had been exposed to asbestos whilst working for two different employers (one of who was uninsured and insolvent) and also whilst working as a self-employed plasterer. The House of Lords had to consider two things: (i) whether the *Fairchild* approach to proof of causation could be applied when the claimant had also been exposed to asbestos whilst self-employed; and (ii) whether the defendants were jointly (liable for all the damage suffered) or severally liable (responsible for their contribution to the risk of the damage occurring). On the first question the House of Lords applied the *Fairchild* approach to proof of causation, but on the second reversed the decision in ruling that liability was several. This meant that like in *Fairchild* the defendant(s) could be liable without proof of causation but unlike *Fairchild* that they would only be liable for a proportion of the damage equivalent to the extent that their negligence had exposed the claimant to the risk of the damage. The claimant's damages were thus reduced by 20 per cent to reflect his own contributory negligence (to cover his exposure whilst self-employed). This decision was swiftly criticised by mesothelioma support groups and trade unions who argued that very sick and dying people would now have to spend precious time and resources trying to establish the relative liabilities of former employers (many of whom were now no longer trading or lacking resources/insurance to meet any award that would be made against them). Pressure was put on government and the Compensation Act 2006 was passed to restore the *Fairchild* position of joint and several liability for mesothelioma cases. The Act applies uniquely to situations where mesothelioma has been contracted after exposure to asbestos.

Sections 3(1) and 3(2) provide that a person who has negligently or in breach of statutory duty causes or permits another person to be exposed to asbestos will be liable for the whole of the damage caused to the victim if they go on to contract mesothelioma even if it is not possible to establish with certainty whether it was this or another exposure that caused them to become ill. Section 3(2)(b) establishes that all those who fall within these sections shall be jointly and severally liable. The purpose of this legislation is to ensure that a person suffering from mesothelioma is able to recover full damages in situation in which he could only establish a case against one of several possible tortfeasors provided that he could establish that his exposure to asbestos at work had created a material increase in the riks that he would develop mesothelioma (*Sienkiewicz v Greif (UK) Ltd* [2011]).

LOSS OF A CHANCE

In *Gregg v Scott* [2005] the House of Lords confirmed the rule that the loss of a chance of recovering from or avoiding some injury or illness is not actionable in tort. The defendant doctor failed to diagnose a lump in the claimant's armpit as cancerous. By the time it had been properly diagnosed and treated, his chances of recovery had been reduced from 40 per cent to 22 per cent. It was held that the claimant could not show on the balance of probabilities (ie that it was more likely than not) that the misdiagnosis had caused him any damage. Lord Nicholls dissented, arguing that the law should recognise the reality of medical practice, which deals in chances of recovery, and not absolute, certain outcomes. As Lord Nicholls pointed out, the current state of the law means that anyone with a chance of recovery less than 50 per cent can never have an action for medical negligence – even when a 49 per cent chance of recovery is reduced by clinical error to zero. In effect, there is no tortious duty to take care in the treatment of such patients.

Lost chances can be compensated in some situations. When assessing damages, the courts routinely compensate lost chances – e.g. the chance that someone might have enjoyed a promotion or bonus at work is compensated on a chance basis, as part of loss of earnings; the claimant does not have to prove that the promotion was more likely to have happened than not. Conversely, damages may be reduced on the basis that the claimant might anyway have contracted in the future a disease triggered by the defendant's tort: e.g. *Smith v Leech Brain* [1961]. More dubiously, *Gregg v Scott* seems to apply only to personal injury, and not pure economic loss. The House of Lords approved *Allied Maples v Simmonds & Simmonds* [1995], where the lost chance of renegotiating a contract was held to be recoverable.

OMISSIONS

If the negligent conduct takes the form of an omission, special difficulties arise. The court must consider what would have happened if the defendant had acted instead of omitting to do so. The issue will then be whether the omission to act made any difference to the outcome. In cases involving special skills, the *Bolam* test, as modified by *Bolitho*, will then apply (*Bolitho v City and Hackney Health Authority* [1997]).

In *Chester v Afshar* [2004] the claimant sued a neurosurgeon after surgery on her spine left her paralysed. It was found that although the surgery had not been performed negligently, the surgeon had failed to give the claimant adequate warning of the 1–2 per cent risk of paralysis that accompanied the operation she was to undergo. Although the claimant would have probably still proceeded with the surgery she contended that she would not have had it straight away. The House of Lords held there to be a causal link between the defendant's failure to warn of the surgery's risk and the damage suffered by the claimant. The 'but for' test was satisfied by the fact that the claimant would not have had the operation when she did if warned of the inherent risk. Lord Steyn justified this departure from traditional causation principles in order to protect the claimant's right of autonomy and dignity, a clear policy decision to bolster the position of informed consent in medical treatment.

INTERVENING ACTS THAT BREAK THE CHAIN OF CAUSATION:
NOVUS ACTUS INTERVENIENS

Sometimes, something can occur between the defendant's act and the claimant's injury which breaks the chain of causation so that the defendant can no longer be said to be liable to the claimant. This is a *novus actus interveniens*.

It was described by Lord Wright in the *The Oropesa* [1943]:

> ... a new cause which disturbs the sequence of events, something which can be described as either unreasonable or extraneous or extrinsic.

The facts of *The Oropesa* [1943] were that two ships collided. The captain of one ship put out to sea in heavy weather in a lifeboat to discuss the situation with the captain of the other ship and was drowned. It was argued that this constituted a *novus actus interveniens*, but this was rejected as it was held that the decision to put out to sea was reasonable in the circumstances.

A rescuer's intervention will not be considered a *novus actus interveniens*, as long as the peril is active, see *Haynes v Harwood* [1935].

The courts have taken quite a restrictive approach to 'unreasonable or extraneous' acts. In *Philco Radio and Television Corp v J Spurling* [1949], a 'foolish or mischievous' act was said not to break the chain of causation between the defendants' negligent misdelivery of highly flammable materials and an explosion at the claimant's premises. Tucker LJ commented that even if the fire had not been started accidentally, the person responsible could not have known of the explosive properties of the material, and so 'the behaviour on her part was not such a conscious act of volition as to relieve the defendants of the liability which arose from their admitted negligence'.

Not every illegal act constitutes a *novus actus interveniens*, as in *Rouse v Squires* [1973], where the court required a reckless, negligent act. The first defendant caused a motorway accident; a second driver, who was driving too fast and failed to keep a proper lookout, collided with the stationary vehicles. The first driver was held to be partially responsible for the additional damage as the intervening conduct had not been so reckless as to constitute a *novus actus*. This approach was followed in *Wright v Lodge* [1993], where the first defendant negligently left her car on the carriageway in thick fog. The second defendant was deemed to be driving recklessly when he collided with the first defendant's car while driving at 60 mph before swerving across the carriageway and crashing into several other cars. It was held that the second driver's recklessness broke the chain of causation and the first defendant could not be held liable for the damage suffered by the other drivers.

Knightley v Johns [1982] is hard to reconcile with *Rouse v Squires* and *Wright v Lodge*, and the differences arise as a result of policy decisions on the part of the court. In the words of Stephenson LJ in *Knightley v Johns*, the court looks at 'common sense rather than logic on the facts and circumstances of each case'.

ACTS OF THE CLAIMANT

The claimant's acts can constitute a *novus actus interveniens*, as in *McKew v Holland and Hannen and Cubitts* [1969], where the defendants had injured the claimant's left leg. One day, as the claimant was descending some stairs he felt that his leg was about to give way, so he jumped down the remaining stairs, thereby injuring his right leg. The claimant's act constituted a *novus actus interveniens* as it had been an unreasonable act in the circumstances.

By contrast, in *Wieland v Cyril Lord Carpets* [1969], the claimant's neck had been injured by the defendants and as a consequence she was required to wear a surgical collar. She fell, as she had been unable to use her bifocal spectacles with her usual skill, and suffered further injuries. The additional injuries were held to be attributable to the defendant's original negligence.

In *Corr v IBC Vehicles* [2008] the House of Lords found that although suicide could be a *novus actus interveniens* if a person took his own life as a conscious decision in the absence of any disabling mental illness, the suicide of the claimant's husband was the result of his depression following a near-fatal accident at work caused by the defendant's negligence. After the accident the claimant's husband had ongoing physical and psychological problems and depression was within the compensational damage that he suffered so the chain of causation was not severed by his suicide.

In *Kirkham v Chief Constable of the Greater Manchester Police* [1990], it was held that the suicide of a prisoner in police custody was not a *novus actus interveniens*. The police were under a duty to guard the prisoner to prevent that type of incident occurring.

This reasoning was approved by the House of Lords in *Reeves v Metropolitan Police Commissioner* [1999], another case in which a prisoner committed suicide in police custody, although on this occasion, unlike *Kirkham*, he was found to have been of sound mind at the time.

REMOTENESS OF DAMAGE

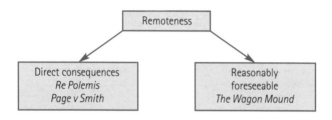

Theoretically, the consequences of conduct are endless; so, even where the defendant has breached a duty, there must be some 'cut off' point beyond which the defendant will not be liable. If a defendant was responsible for his actions *ad infinitum* human activity would be unreasonably hampered.

Since 1850, there have been two competing views as to the test for remoteness of damage:

- Consequences are too remote if a reasonable man would not have foreseen them: *The Wagon Mound (No 1)* [1967].

- The defendant is liable for all the direct consequences of his act suffered by the claimant, whether a reasonable man would have foreseen them or not, no matter how unusual or unexpected: *Re Polemis v Furness Withy & Co Ltd* [1921].

The Wagon Mound lays down the rule that foreseeability of damage is the test not only for the imposition of a duty of care but also for remoteness of damage. Remember, in this context we are looking at liability for the extent of damage, not whether a duty exists.

> ▶ OVERSEAS TANKSHIP (UK) LTD v MORTS DOCK &
> ENGINEERING CO LTD (THE WAGON MOUND) [1961]

Basic facts

A large quantity of fuel oil was negligently discharged into Sydney Harbour from the defendant's ship. The oil drifted over to the claimant's wharf where another ship was being welded. After taking expert advice the claimants were assured that it was safe to resume welding, but two days later the oil caught fire and the wharf and ships being repaired were damaged by the fire. At first instance and on appeal the claimant was successful on application of the directness test from *Re Polemis*. The Privy Council reversed the decision.

Relevance

The fact that some of the damage (to the slipways) was foreseeable did not make the defendants liable for the unforeseeable fire. The test for remoteness of damage was whether the kind of damage sustained was reasonably foreseeable. The Privy Council was also of the opinion that the directness test for remoteness of damage from *Re Polemis* should no longer be used.

MANNER OF OCCURRENCE OF DAMAGE NEED NOT BE FORESEEABLE

If the type of injury is foreseeable then the manner in which it occurs need not be foreseeable: *Hughes v Lord Advocate* [1963], but note that this case was distinguished in *Doughty v Turner Manufacturing Co Ltd* [1964].

TYPE OF INJURY MUST BE FORESEEABLE

In *Tremain v Pike* [1969], the claimant was a herdsman who was employed by the defendants. He contracted Weil's Disease, which is an extremely rare disease, caught by coming into contact with rats' urine. It was held that although injury through food contamination was foreseeable, a 'rare disease' was a different type of injury and was not therefore foreseeable.

However, the House of Lords in *Page v Smith* [1995] awarded damages for psychiatric injury even though only physical injury was foreseeable. It was held that, in the case of primary victims, there should be no distinction between physical and psychiatric injury.

Again it was said by the Court of Appeal *obiter* in *Giblett v P and N E Murray Ltd* [1999] that where physical injury is foreseeable in an accident, damages for consequent psychiatric injury were recoverable in principle. Foreseeability of psychological harm need not be shown. On the facts of the case, no causal link was established.

THE EXTENT OF THE DAMAGE NEED NOT BE FORESEEABLE: THIN SKULL RULE

Provided the *type* of injury is foreseeable, the defendant will be liable for its full extent even if that is greater than could have been foreseen due to some peculiar susceptibility of the claimant, for example, a thin skull.

So, in *Bradford v Robinson Rentals* [1967], a lorry driver was subject to extreme cold and suffered frost-bite as a result. The defendants were liable for the frost-bite, even though this was greater than could have been foreseen, because the type of injury was foreseeable. This can be contrasted with *Tremain v Pike* [1969], where the type of injury had not been foreseeable.

IMPECUNIOSITY OF THE CLAIMANT

There is a duty in tort to mitigate one's loss, that is, not to increase one's loss unnecessarily. Problems arise where the claimant has insufficient means to be able to afford to mitigate his loss. The courts have not always been consistent in their approach. In *Liesbosch Dredger v SS Edison* [1933], the claimants had been put to much greater expense in fulfilling a contract because they were too poor to buy a substitute dredger for the one which had been damaged by the defendants. It was held that the claimants' impecuniosity had to be disregarded and they were unable to recover the additional expenses.

This can be contrasted with more recent cases, such as *Dodd Properties Ltd v Canterbury City Council* [1980] and *Martindale v Duncan* [1973], where delays in repair caused by impecuniosity and the cost of substitute hire vehicles were allowed. It was said in *Mattocks v Mann* [1992] that *Liesbosch Dredger* was constantly being reviewed in the light of changed circumstances, and hire charges were again allowed.

In *Alcoa Minerals v Broderick* [2000], the Privy Council confirmed that *Liesbosch Dredger* laid down no absolute rule that damages attributable to impecuniosity cannot be recovered. On the facts of the case, it had been foreseeable that the claimant would not be able to afford to repair a damaged building, and thus his delay in carrying out the repairs was quite reasonable and the additional cost of repair could be recovered. The House of Lords held in *Lagden v O'Connor* [2003] that there is no special rule about consequential losses caused by impecuniosity. These are recoverable, provided they are foreseeable, on ordinary *Wagon Mound* principles.

VICARIOUS LIABILITY

Vicarious liability is where one person is made liable for the torts of another. Although the most common relationship in which vicarious liability arises is that between employer and employee, it may also arise in other circumstances, but these are of less importance. They include principal and agent, business partners and vehicle owners and delegated drivers. Vicarious liability is thus a tort of strict liability (no need to prove fault) and must be clearly differentiated from primary liability.

Three conditions must be met in order to impose vicarious liability on a defendant:

(i) There must be an employer/employee relationship.
(ii) A tort must have been committed by an employee.
(iii) The employee must have been acting in the course of employment when the tort was committed.

Many justifications have been advanced for allowing vicarious liability, in *Bazley v Curry* [1999] McLachlin J referred to two key justifications, 'fair compensation' and 'deterrence', proposed by Fleming in *Law of Torts*.

The first of these has a strong justice element running through it. Essentially the argument is that the employer should take the risk of any harm because they stand to take the benefit of the activity that creates the risk. In both *Dubai Aluminium v Salaam* [2002] and *Majrowski v Guy's & St Thomas's NHS Trust* [2006] it was stated that this argument does not rely on there being anything inherently wrong with the creation of the risk, that the risk might just be a normal by-product of a lawful enterprise.

The deterrence argument relies on the control employers have over employees not only as to who is employed, but what tasks they are required to do and how they are to be done. As McLachlin J put it in *Bazley v Curry* [1999]:

> Beyond the narrow band of employer conduct that attracts direct liability in negligence lies a vast area where imaginative and efficient administration and supervision can reduce the risk that the employer has introduced into the community.

Vicarious liability is not restricted to common law claims, in *Majrowski v Guy's & St Thomas's NHS Trust* [2006] the employer was held vicariously liable for a breach of statutory duty imposed on the employee by the Protection from Harassment Act 1997; however, it is frequently discussed in negligence cases. In some instances, on the same facts, employers can both be vicariously liable for tort(s) committed by an employee and primarily liable themselves in negligence if they have breached a duty of care that they owed to the claimant(s).

EMPLOYER/EMPLOYEE RELATIONSHIP

Although employers may be vicariously liable for the torts committed by employees, they are not usually liable for the torts of independent contractors. In *Ferguson v John Dawson & Partners (Contractors) Ltd* [1976] the court held that although the express intentions of the parties as to the nature of their working relationship might be an important factor it was not conclusive and the court would look at the nature of the relationship as being determinative of whether it was a 'contract of service' (employer/employee) or 'contract for services' (independent contractor) relationship.

In *Mersey Docks and Harbour Board v Coggins & Griffith (Liverpool) Ltd* [1946] a mobile crane and driver had been hired out by the Mersey Docks & Harbour Board to a firm of stevedores. The contract stipulated that the driver was to be an employee of the stevedores but the Board continued to pay his wages and retained the right to terminate his employment. Whilst working for the stevedores the driver negligently injured the claimant. In determining who was vicariously liable, the House of Lords decided that although several factors must be considered, the determining one was who had ultimate control over the way in which the driver performed his work. The Board were found to have this control and so were liable irrespective of the contract under which the driver was rented out.

The 'control' test had held sway for some time but in more modern working arrangements it became difficult to apply. In *Stevenson, Jordan and Harrison Ltd v McDonald & Evans* [1952] Lord Denning suggested the 'business integration' test: a worker would be an employee if their work was an integral part of the business rather than just an accessory to it. This test was proven too vague in practice. A variant of it, where the worker was in business on their own account, developed. In *Ready Mixed Concrete (SE) Ltd v Minister of Pensions* [1968] the court found that there were a number of relevant factors to be taken into account and one of these was: who bore the financial risk? This approach was also followed in *Market Investigations Ltd v Minister of Social Security* [1968].

▶ VIASYSTEMS LTD v THERMAL TRANSFER LTD [2005]

Basic facts

The first defendants were hired to install air-conditioning in the claimant's factory. They sub-contracted out the work to the second defendants who contracted with the third defendants to provide fitters on a labour only basis. One of the fitters supplied by the third defendant negligently damaged the factory's sprinkler system by crawling through a duct that he should not have attempted. The court had to decide which of the employers was vicariously liable for the damage caused by the fitter's negligence.

Relevance

The approach taken was to ask who was responsible for preventing the negligent act; it was found that both the second and third defendants were entitled to exercise control over the fitter and what he was doing. The second and third defendants were both held to be vicariously liable.

IN THE COURSE OF EMPLOYMENT

In deciding whether the tort was committed in the course of employment the starting point has traditionally been the 'Salmond' test:

A master is not responsible for a wrongful act done by his servant unless it is done in the course of employment. It is deemed to be done so if it is either (a) a wrongful act authorised by the master, or (b) a wrongful and unauthorised mode of doing some act authorised by the master.

Some acts fall clearly outside of the scope of the employment. In *Beard v London General Omnibus Co* [1900] the employers of a bus conductor were found not to be vicariously liable for the injury he caused to another when trying to turn a bus around because he was not employed to drive buses. However, in *Limpus v London General Omnibus Co* [1862] despite written instructions not to race with or obstruct buses from other companies, the driver did just that, causing an accident as a result of his negligence. Despite the explicit instructions not to race his bus, the driver was employed to drive the bus. He was doing an authorised act in an unauthorised way so the bus company was vicariously liable. Even if an employee is doing their job negligently it does not take them outside the course of their employment. In *Century Insurance Co v Northern Ireland Road Transport Board* [1942] the employers of a petrol tanker driver were held vicariously liable for his negligence in smoking whilst unloading petrol. He discarded a lighted match which caused an explosion and fire.

In *Twine v Bean's Express Ltd* [1946] the defendant's employee gave a lift to the claimant's husband despite being prohibited from giving lifts. There was even a notice on the side of the vehicle stating who could be an authorised passenger. The claimant's husband was killed as a result of the employee's negligent driving. The defendants were not held vicariously liable because at the time of the accident the driver was doing an unauthorised act. If the unauthorised act is performed in the course of promoting the employer's business then it may fall within the course of employment *Rose v Plenty* [1976].

The modern approach to considering the course of employment question is to look at whether the torts committed were so closely associated with the employee's duties that it would be fair and just to hold the employers liable.

> ▶ **LISTER v HESLEY HALL LTD [2001]**
>
> Basic facts
> The claimants had been resident in a boarding house owned and run by the defendants. The warden employed by the defendants systematically abused the children in his care. The defendants were not found to be primarily negligent in their selection and monitoring of the warden.
>
> Relevance
> The House of Lords decided that the defendants had entrusted the children to the care of the warden and that his abuse of them was inextricably interwoven with the carrying out of his duties. Since his torts had been so closely connected with his employment it was fair and just to hold the defendants vicariously liable.

This decision has been followed in *Mattis v Pollock* [2003] by the Court of Appeal and also in *Gravil v Caroll* [2008] where a tortious assault by one rugby player on a member of the opposing team during a match was so closely connected with his employment by the rugby club that it was fair and just to hold the club vicariously liable for injury to the opponent.

EMPLOYER'S INDEMNITY

Vicarious liability is established if (a) the employee has committed a tort and (b) this occurred during the course of his employment. As both the employee and the employer thus incur tortious liability, they are joint tortfeasors which means that the employer may be able to recover some of the cost of paying damages to the claimant from the employee. This may fall within section 1(1) of the Civil Liability Contribution Act 1978 which provides that one defendant (i.e. the employer) may recover damages from another defendant who is responsible for the harm or loss caused (i.e. the employee) on the basis of what is 'just and reasonable'. This could mean that the employee has to pay the employer the entire amount of damages if the court felt that the employer, although vicariously liable for the employee's tort, was wholly blameless.

Lister v Romford Ice & Cold Storage Co [1957] set out the common law position, holding that an employer who has been held vicariously liable for an employee's negligence is entitled to pursue an indemnity (the full cost of the damages) from the employee to recover any damages paid if the loss or injury was caused by the employee's breach of contract.

EMPLOYERS' LIABILITY

Vicarious liability covers situations in which the employer is made liable for the torts committed by his employees. This should not be confused by employers' liability in which the employer is liable in tort for harm or loss caused to his employees. Such liability may arise under common law or statute.

At common law, every employer is under a duty to take reasonable care to ensure the safety of his employees. This was said to have four different elements in *Wilsons and Clyde Coal Co Ltd v English* [1937]:

■ A duty to provide safe premises and a safe place to work.

■ A duty to provide safe plant, equipment and materials.

■ A duty to provide a safe system of work and safe working practices.

■ A duty to provide competent staff as colleagues.

This common law duty is supplemented by a whole raft of statutory provisions, some of which apply to particular types of work or places of employment such as the Minerals Working (Offshore Installations) Act 1971 and some of which are of more general application such as the Health and Safety at Work etc Act 1974.

You should now be confident that you would be able to tick all of the boxes on the checklist at the beginning of this chapter. To check your knowledge of Negligence why not visit the companion website and take the Multiple Choice Question test. Check your understanding of the terms and vocabulary used in this chapter with the flashcard glossary.

2

Occupiers' liability

LIABILITY UNDER THE OCCUPIERS' LIABILITY ACT 1957

The law of occupiers' liability exists to ensure that an occupier's land is not dangerous to others. It is governed by statute law which was introduced to clarify the pre-existing common law. The original *Occupiers' Liability Act 1957* which protected lawful visitors to land was joined by the *Occupiers' Liability Act 1984* which extended liability to injury suffered by trespassers.

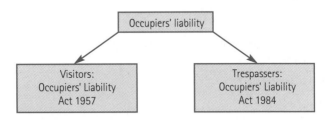

WHO IS AN 'OCCUPIER' FOR THE PURPOSES OF THE ACT?

Common law rules apply

The 1957 Act does not define what constitutes an occupier but stipulates that the rules of the common law shall apply (s 1(2)).

The test is one of control and not exclusive occupation

▶ WHEAT v E LACON & CO LTD [1966]

Basic facts

The defendants owned a public house and the manager and his wife occupied the upper floor. The manager's wife was allowed to take paying guests, and one of these guests had an accident on the staircase leading to the upper floor. It was held that the defendants were occupiers of the upper floor as they exercised residuary control.

Relevance

The basic test for an occupier is one of control over the premises. There can be more than one occupier of premises at any given time.

It is not necessary to be present on the premises

In *Harris v Birkenhead Corporation* [1976], the local authority had issued a notice of compulsory purchase order and notice of entry but had not taken possession. They were held to be occupiers for the purposes of the Act.

WHO IS A 'VISITOR' FOR THE PURPOSES OF THE ACT?

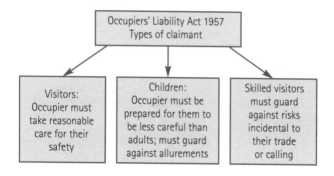

Occupiers' Liability Act 1957
Types of claimant

Visitors:
Occupier must take reasonable care for their safety

Children:
Occupier must be prepared for them to be less careful than adults; must guard against allurements

Skilled visitors must guard against risks incidental to their trade or calling

General category of visitor

The Act replaces the old common law distinctions between 'invitees' and 'licensees' with a general category of 'visitor'.

Express and implied permission

A visitor is someone who has express or implied permission to be on the land. So, a visitor is either someone who has been expressly requested to enter onto premises, or someone who has implied permission to be there.

- *Knowledge of presence does not imply permission.* The fact that the occupier knows of the claimant's presence or has failed to take steps to prevent entry does not mean that the occupier has given permission to enter, see *Edwards v Railway Executive* [1952].

- *Rules the same for children but may be implied permission.* Knowledge that a track is constantly used by children, together with a failure to take any steps to indicate that passage is not permitted, does amount to an implied permission, see *Lowery v Walker* [1911].

- *Implied permission to enter must be exercised properly.* It was held in *Harvey v Plymouth City Council* [2010] that a land owner gives implied permission for people to come onto their land and behave in a normal manner and to exercise the rights of a the visitor in an ordinary way and that duty to ensure that land was safe for visitors was limited to this ordinary use of the land.

- *Entering premises to communicate with occupier does amount to implied permission.* A person entering with the purpose of communicating with the occupier will have implied permission, for example, someone asking directions, the postman, roundsman, etc.

- *Entering premises to exercise a right conferred by law amounts to implied permission.* Section 2(6) stipulates that anyone entering premises for any purpose in the exercise of a right conferred by law is a lawful visitor, for example, police with search warrants and officials empowered by statute to enter premises.

- *Exercising a public right of way does not constitute implied permission.* A person exercising a public right of way has no claim under the 1957 Act because such a person was not an 'invitee' or 'licensee' at common law.

  In *Greenhalgh v British Railway Board* [1969], a railway bridge was built by the defendant's predecessor in title in 1873. In 1950, a housing estate was built on either side of the railway bridge and the bridge was used to connect the two. The claimant was injured when he stepped into a pothole. It was held that the claimant was exercising a right of way and was not a 'visitor'.

- *Statutory access to land.* Those enjoying access to land under the National Parks and Access to the Countryside Act 1949 or the Countryside and Rights of Way Act 2000 do not enjoy the status of a visitor under the 1957 Act. Amendments to the Occupiers' Liability Act 1984 (below) state that landowners will not be liable to those entering under the 2000 Act if the injury is due to natural features of the landscape. Moreover, in considering the extent of an occupier's duty to such entrants, the court must not place an undue burden on the occupier, and must take into account 'the importance of maintaining the character of the countryside, including features of historic, traditional or archaeological interest'.

THE COMMON DUTY OF CARE

The 1957 Act states that a common duty of care is owed by an occupier to all visitors except insofar as he has extended, restricted, excluded or modified his duty.

The common duty of care is the duty to take such care as is reasonable to see that the visitor will be reasonably safe in using the premises for the purpose for which he is invited by the occupier to be there (s 2(2)).

Standard of care

The same standard of care applies as that which applies in ordinary negligence.

Guidelines

The 1957 Act provides guidelines in the application of the common duty of care. Section 2(3) provides that the circumstances relevant for the purpose include the degree of care and want of care which would ordinarily be looked for in such a visitor, so that (for example) in proper cases:

- an occupier must be prepared for children to be less careful than adults;

- an occupier is entitled to expect that a person in the exercise of his calling will appreciate and guard against any special risks ordinarily incidental to his trade or calling.

Children

An occupier must be prepared for children to be less careful than adults. In *Moloney v Lambeth LBC* [1966], the occupier was liable when a four-year-old boy fell through a gap in railings protecting a stairwell, when an adult could not have fallen through the gap. However, in *Keown v Coventry Healthcare NHS Trust* [2006] the Court of Appeal found that whilst an occupier must be prepared for children to be less careful than adults, the extent of the occupier's liability depends on the circumstances of the case and is a question of fact and degree. An 11-year-old boy had been injured after falling from the outside of a fire escape on which he had been climbing. After finding no defect or disrepair in the fire escape, the Court of Appeal found that the only danger 'arose from the activity of the claimant in choosing to climb up the outside, knowing it was dangerous to do so'. It would not be right to ignore a child's choice to indulge in a dangerous activity merely because he was a child in every case.

■ *Allurements.* An occupier must take precautions against children being attracted by allurements. In *Glasgow Corporation v Taylor* [1922], a seven-year-old boy ate poisonous berries on a visit to a botanical garden. It was held that the occupiers were liable as they knew that the berries were poisonous and they had made no attempt to fence the berries off.

■ *Definition of allurements.* Allurements were defined by Hamilton LJ in *Latham v R Johnson and Nephew Ltd* [1913] as something involving the idea of 'concealment and surprise, of an appearance of safety under circumstances cloaking a reality of danger'. So, in that case, a child playing with a heap of stones had no remedy, as stones do not involve any element of allurement. In *Jolley v Sutton London Borough Council* [2000], the House of Lords ruled that a boat in a dangerous condition was an allurement to a 14-year-old.

In *Phipps v Rochester Corporation* [1955], a trench that was not concealed was held not to be an allurement; and in *Simkiss v Rhondda BC* [1982], there was no concealed danger in sliding down a steep slope on a blanket.

Skilled visitors

An occupier is entitled to expect that a person in the exercise of his calling will appreciate and guard against any special risks ordinarily incidental to his trade or calling.

In *Roles v Nathan* [1963], two chimney sweeps died from carbon monoxide poisoning while cleaning the flue of a boiler. They had been warned not to continue working while the boiler was alight. The occupier was held not to be liable as, first, the sweeps had been warned of the danger and, secondly, it was reasonable to expect a specialist to appreciate and guard against the dangers arising from the very defect that he had been called in to deal with.

■ *The risk must be incidental to the trade or calling.* In *Bird v King Line Ltd* [1970], it was held that the risks of working on a ship did not include falling on refuse which was carelessly left on the deck.

■ *Occupier liability to skilled rescuers.* In *Ogwo v Taylor* [1988], the occupier negligently started a fire and was liable to a fireman injured in the blaze where the fire fighting operation had been carried out with due care.

Independent contractors

It will be a defence for the occupier to show that the defective state of the premises was caused by the faulty execution of any work of construction, repair or maintenance by an independent contractor, provided that (s 2(4)(b)):

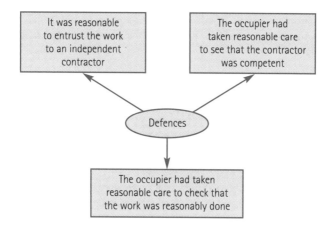

It was reasonable to entrust the work to an independent contractor

The occupier had taken reasonable care to see that the contractor was competent

Defences

The occupier had taken reasonable care to check that the work was reasonably done

Reasonable to entrust work to a contractor

Whether it was reasonable to entrust the work to a contractor and the nature of the work to be done depends on the circumstances.

The more complex the work, the more reasonable it will be to entrust it to a contractor. Thus, in *Haseldine v CA Daw & Son Ltd* [1941], an occupier was not liable for the negligence of an independent contractor in maintaining a lift in a block of flats. This can be contrasted with *Woodward v Mayor of Hastings* [1944], where the occupiers were liable for the negligence of a cleaner in leaving a step in an icy condition. Cleaning a step does not require any particular skill.

DISCHARGE OF THE DUTY OF CARE

Warning

Section 2(4)(a) provides that an occupier can discharge his duty to a visitor by giving a warning of the danger that in all the circumstances allows the visitor to be reasonably safe.

The test for determining whether a warning was adequate is a subjective one. A written warning will not be adequate in the case of someone who is blind, or who cannot read or speak English.

In *Staples v West Dorset District Council* [1995], it was held that an occupier had not been negligent when the council had failed to provide a warning and the danger was obvious. In such circumstances, a warning would not have told the visitor anything he did not already know and would not have affected his conduct.

Acceptance of the risk

Section 2(5) provides that an occupier does not have an obligation to a visitor in respect of risks willingly accepted by the visitor.

In *Simms v Leigh RFC Ltd* [1969], the claimant had accepted the risks of playing on a rugby league ground which conformed to the bylaws of the Rugby League.

■ *Knowledge of specific risk.* In *White v Blackmore* [1972], it was held that it was insufficient to show that the claimant knew that jalopy car racing was dangerous; it was necessary to show that the claimant had consented to the specific risk that made that particular track dangerous.

Exclusion of liability

Section 2(1) provides that an occupier is able to 'exclude, restrict or modify his duty'. In *Ashdown v Samuel Williams & Sons Ltd* [1957], the Court of Appeal accepted that a notice was sufficient to exclude liability. In *White v Blackmore* [1972], notices put at the entrance to the field were sufficient to exclude liability.

■ *Unfair Contract Terms Act 1977.* The Unfair Contract Terms Act (UCTA) has greatly restricted the occupier's ability to exclude his liability.

■ *Premises used for business premises.* As far as premises used for business purposes are concerned, the occupier is unable to exclude liability for death and personal injury.

Exclusion of liability for other types of loss must satisfy the reasonableness test contained in s 11 of UCTA.

■ *Premises used for private purposes.* Occupiers of premises which are not in business use can exclude liability only if such exclusion is reasonable.

■ *Remoteness.* The test for remoteness under the 1957 Act is the same as applies to a common law claim for negligence (*Jolley v Sutton London Borough Council* [2000]).

OCCUPIERS' LIABILITY TO TRESPASSERS

COMMON LAW RULE

At common law, the original rule was that there was a mere duty not to injure a trespasser deliberately or recklessly, see *Addie v Dumbreck* [1929].

▶ BRITISH RAILWAYS BOARD v HERRINGTON [1972]

Basic facts

The six-year-old claimant used a gap in a fence to trespass on the defendant's land and was badly injured when he touched the electrified rail. The defendants new that children had been seen on the line in the past but had taken no action.

Relevance

It was held that an occupier was under a duty to act humanely towards trespassers – when a reasonable man knowing the physical facts which the occupier actually knew would appreciate that a trespasser's presence at the point and time of danger was so likely that, in all the circumstances it would be inhumane not to give effective warning of the danger.

OCCUPIERS' LIABILITY ACT 1984

The Occupiers' Liability Act 1984 replaces the common law to determine whether an occupier owes a duty to persons other than visitors.

Under s 1(3), a duty is owed by the occupier if:

(a) he is aware of the danger or has reasonable grounds to believe that it exists;

(b) he knows or has reasonable grounds to believe that the other person is in the vicinity of the danger concerned or that he may come into the vicinity of the danger (in either case, whether the other has lawful authority for being in that vicinity or not); and

(c) the risk is one against which, in all the circumstances of the case, he may reasonably be expected to offer the other some protection.

In *Donoghue v Folkstone Properties* [2003], the claimant was injured when he dived into the sea on Boxing Day. It was held that his presence in the harbour at that time of year was entirely unexpected, and thus s 1(3)(b) was not satisfied, and the defendants owed no duty under the 1984 Act.

In *Ratcliff v McConnell* [1998], the Court of Appeal decided that a student who was seriously injured when he dived into a swimming pool at 2 am when it was locked had consented to run the risk of injury under s 1(6) of the 1984 Act, which provides that no duty is owed in respect of risks that were 'willingly accepted'.

▶ TOMLINSON v CONGLETON BOROUGH COUNCIL [2003]

Basic facts

The respondent was seriously injured after misjudging a dive from a standing position, in the shallows of a lake owned by the appellant council. Warning signs and rangers employed by the council had been ineffective in preventing swimmers from using the lake in large numbers during the summer months, as the council certainly knew. The respondent argued that the warning signs and other precautionary measures did not discharge the council's duty under s 1(3) of the 1984 Act. The House of Lords allowed the council's appeal and held that there was no duty of care owed.

Relevance

There was no risk to the respondent from the state of the premises or from anything done or omitted to be done by the appellant. The risk of injury from diving into shallow water was obvious and not one against which the appellant might reasonably have been expected to offer the respondent protection under s 1(3) of the 1984 Act.

In *Tomlinson v Congleton Borough Council* [2003], the House of Lords rejected the argument that further steps should have been taken to discourage bathers, such as planting the beach areas at the margin of the lake with reeds, to render the water inaccessible. It was said that the social value of the existing amenity that would be lost by such modifications must be weighed against the value of accident prevention. Moreover, Lord Hoffmann said, 'I think it will be extremely rare for an occupier of land to be under a duty to prevent people from taking risks which are inherent in the activities they freely choose to undertake upon the land'.

DISCHARGE OF THE DUTY

Warning

Section 1(5) of the 1984 Act provides that the duty may be discharged by taking such steps as are reasonable in all the circumstances to warn of the danger concerned, or to discourage people from incurring the risk.

The House of Lords agreed in *Tomlinson v Congleton BC* [2003]. A duty to protect against obvious risks would arise only in the absence of an informed choice to run those risks, such as the inability of children to perceive risk. A concealed danger would be a different matter. Lord Hobhouse commented that the law did not require the coastline and other beauty spots to be littered with warning notices because of the indulgence of 'a foolhardy few' in activities dangerous only to themselves.

OCCUPIERS' LIABILITY

EXCLUSION OF LIABILITY

The 1984 Act is silent on the question whether the duty can be excluded with regard to trespassers. It has been argued that it is not possible to exclude liability to a trespasser as it is a minimal duty.

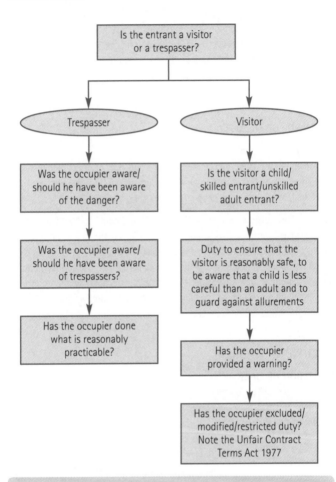

You should now be confident that you would be able to tick all of the boxes on the checklist at the beginning of this chapter. To check your knowledge of Occupiers' liability why not visit the companion website and take the Multiple Choice Question test. Check your understanding of the terms and vocabulary used in this chapter with the flashcard glossary.

Torts relating to land

PRIVATE NUISANCE

Nuisance may be categorised as private nuisance, which affects an individual or a particular property, or public nuisance, which affects a broader group of people. It is one way in which the law of tort protects a peaceful existence free from outside interference.

BASES OF LIABILITY:

Negligence	Private nuisance	Public nuisance	*Rylands v Fletcher* [1868]
Fault: breach of duty which caused injury	Fault: unreasonable use of land	Can be a tort of strict liability: *Wringe v Cohen* [1939]; *Tarry v Ashton* [1876]; otherwise interference with rights of public	Strict liability

THE RELATIONSHIP BETWEEN PRIVATE NUISANCE AND PUBLIC NUISANCE

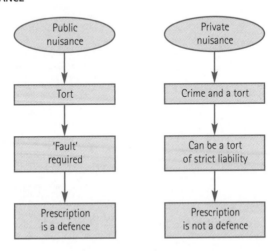

There tends to be confusion between public and private nuisance. Public nuisance is usually a crime covering a number of interferences with rights of the public at large, such as brothel keeping, selling impure food and obstructing public highways. It is not tortious unless an individual proves that he has suffered particular damage beyond that suffered by the rest of the community.

Private nuisance is an unlawful interference with the use or enjoyment of land, or some right over or in connection with it.

At one time, the law of private nuisance seemed to be moving away from solely restraining activities which affected enjoyment of land. In *Khorasandjian v Bush* [1993], the claimant was granted an injunction not only in respect of harassing telephone calls at home, but also for harassment at work and in the street.

The House of Lords in *Hunter v Canary Wharf* [1997] rejected this approach and confined nuisance to its traditional boundaries. Lord Hoffmann emphasised, in that case, that it is a tort relating to land.

> ### ▶ HUNTER v CANARY WHARF [1997]
>
> **Basic facts**
> Several hundred claimants complained that their television reception was blighted by the presence of the 235-metre high Canary Wharf Tower. Some of the claimants had proprietary interests but others had no property interest in the places that they inhabited. The House of Lords had to answer two questions: (i) is a property interest a prerequisite to sue in private nuisance?; (ii) is impairment of television reception by a physical obstruction a nuisance?
>
> **Relevance**
> (i) holding a property interest in land is necessary to sue in private nuisance; (ii) building between a transmitter and other properties was not actionable as an interference with the use and enjoyment of land.

However, private nuisance has been held to extend to damage to a floating barge moored in a river (*Crown River Cruises Ltd v Kimbolton Fireworks Ltd*

[1996]). Since the barge was in use as a mooring, it was so attached for the purpose of the better use and enjoyment of the claimant's mooring right and, therefore, sufficient to sustain an action for private nuisance.

Public nuisance is different from private nuisance as it is not necessarily connected with the user of land. Public nuisance is usually a crime, although it can be a tort. To make matters even more confusing, the same incident can be both a public and a private nuisance.

TYPES OF PRIVATE NUISANCE
Private nuisance is an unlawful interference with the use or enjoyment of land, or some right over or in connection with it.

What is unlawful falls to be decided after the event itself. Most activities which give rise to claims in nuisance are in themselves lawful. It is only when the activity interferes with another's enjoyment of land to such an extent that it is a nuisance that it becomes unlawful.

Examples of private nuisance
It was said by Lord Wright that 'the forms that nuisance take are protean'. That is to say that there are many different forms of private nuisance. Examples would be as follows:

■ Encroachment on the claimant's land, see *Davey v Harrow Corporation* [1957].

■ Physical damage to the claimant's land, see *Sedleigh-Denfield v O'Callaghan* [1940].

■ Interference with the claimant's use or enjoyment of land through smells, smoke, dust, noise, etc, see *Halsey v Esso Petroleum Co Ltd* [1961].

■ Interference with an easement or profit.

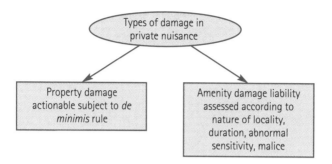

PHYSICAL DAMAGE

As a general rule, nuisance is not actionable of itself and actual damage must be proved, subject to the following exceptions:

- where a presumption of damage can be made, for example, by building a cornice so that it projects over the claimant's land, it may be presumed that damage will be caused to the claimant's land by rain water dripping from the cornice onto the land;

- interference with an easement, *profit à prendre* (right to take profits from land) or right of access where there has been acquiescence in certain circumstances.

So, private nuisance is concerned with balancing the competing claims of neighbours to use their property as they think fit. However, a distinction must be made between physical damage to property, where such conduct will, subject to the *de minimis* rule, be a nuisance, and personal discomfort or amenity damage, where the judge will consider many factors to determine the balance.

If the conduct complained of causes physical damage to the claimant's property, this will amount to nuisance (subject to any defence available). In *St Helens Smelting Co v Tipping* [1865], Lord Westbury said that an 'occupier is entitled to expect protection from physical damage no matter where he lives'.

AMENITY DAMAGE

Amenity damage is interference such as noise, smells, dust and vibrations which will interfere with use and enjoyment of land without physically damaging the property.

In the case of amenity damage, the degree of interference has to be measured against the surrounding circumstances.

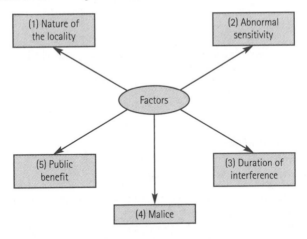

(1) Nature of the locality

This is an important determinant of what constitutes nuisance in the case of amenity damage. As was said in *St Helens Smelting Co v Tipping* [1865], 'one should not expect the clean air of the Lake District in an industrial town such as St Helens'. The claimant's estate was located in a manufacturing area. Fumes from a copper smelting works damaged the trees on the estate. The distinction was made between physical damage and amenity damage, particularly the nature of the surrounding area and locality.

Interesting questions of locality were raised in *Halsey v Esso Petroleum Co Ltd* [1961]. The claimant's house was in a zone that was classified as residential for planning purposes. The defendant's oil depot was across the road in an industrial zone. There was a combination of physical and amenity damage:

▪ acid smuts from the defendant's depot damaged paintwork on the claimant's car, clothing and washing on the line;

▪ there was a nauseating smell;

▪ noise from the boilers caused the claimant's windows and doors to vibrate and prevented him from sleeping. There was also noise from the delivery tankers at night.

The damage to the clothing on washing line etc constituted physical damage and was recoverable. Before allowing recovery for the intangible damage, the locality had to be taken into account. Trifling inconveniences were disregarded but the locality set the measure of what was acceptable, and the interference substantially exceeded the standards of the surrounding neighbourhood.

In *Laws v Florinplace Ltd* [1981], the defendants opened a sex centre and cinema club which showed explicit sex acts. Local residents sought an injunction. It was held that the use constituted a private nuisance.

Similarly, in *Thompson-Schwab v Costaki* [1956], the claimant lived in a respectable residential street in the West End of London. The defendant used a house in the same street for the purposes of prostitution. It was held that, having regard to the character of the neighbourhood, the defendant's use of the property constituted a nuisance.

However, the character of a neighbourhood can change over the years, and a more modern approach is for the court to ask whether the acts complained of are more than can be tolerated in modern living conditions. If so, they will constitute a nuisance, see *Blackburn v ARC Ltd* [1997].

In the public nuisance case of *Gillingham BC v Medway (Chatham) Dock Co Ltd* [1992], it was held that the nature of a locality can be changed through planning permission.

In *Wheeler v Saunders* [1995], it was held that a local authority had no jurisdiction to authorise a nuisance, save in so far as it had the power to permit a change in the character of the neighbourhood and the nuisance resulted inevitably from the change of use.

In *Murdoch v Glacier Metal Co Ltd* [1998], excess noise from a nearby factory above World Health Organisation levels was not actionable nuisance. Allowance had to be made for the character of the neighbourhood, which was next to a busy bypass.

(2) Abnormal sensitivity

Personal discomfort is not to be judged by the standards of the claimant but must be made by reference to the standards of any ordinary person who might occupy the claimant's property. It must be an 'inconvenience materially interfering with the ordinary comfort physically of human existence, not merely according to elegant and dainty modes and habits of living but according to plain and sober and simple notions among the English people', *per* Knight Bruce VC in *Walter v Selfe* [1851].

Consequently, a vicar who was put off his sermons in *Heath v Mayor of Brighton* [1908] by a low hum from the defendant's electricity works was being abnormally sensitive, particularly as he had been the only person annoyed and it had not stopped anyone from attending church.

■ *Abnormal sensitivity and physical damage.* In the same way, a defendant will not be liable for physical damage to property caused because of its exceptionally delicate nature. A man cannot increase the liabilities of his neighbour by applying his own property to special uses.

In *Robinson v Kilvert* [1889], the claimant occupied a basement in the ground floor of the defendant's building and stored brown paper there. The defendant's boiler had an adverse effect on the claimant's goods, although it would not have affected any other type of paper. The claimant failed to get an injunction because of the exceptionally delicate trade that he was carrying on.

■ *Changing nature of use.* *Bridlington Relay Ltd v Yorkshire Electricity Board* [1965] is an illustration of how ideas of 'exceptionally delicate trade' might change. The claimants were in business relaying sound and television broadcasts and the defendant's power lines interfered with their transmissions. It was held that the claimants were carrying on an exceptionally delicate trade.

For some time, it was thought that *Bridlington Relay Ltd* would be decided differently if it came before a court today, not least because television ownership has become much more widespread since the case was decided.

However, in *Hunter v Canary Wharf* [1997], the presence of the Canary Wharf tower interfered with the claimants' television reception but the House of Lords held that they could not succeed in private nuisance. It was not ruled out that interference with television could never be actionable nuisance, but at present it seems unlikely.

On the other hand, if the defendant's activities would have interfered with the ordinary use of the land, he will be liable notwithstanding the claimant's abnormal sensitivity. In *McKinnon Industries Ltd v Walker* [1951], the Privy Council held that once substantial interference is proved, the remedies for interference will extend to a sensitive and delicate operation.

(3) Duration of interference

Interference of a temporary or occasional nature may cause annoyance but an injunction will rarely be granted. The temporary duration of the alleged nuisance is one factor to be taken into account and the judge will conclude that it is the price of social existence that neighbours suffer temporary annoyance at various times, such as during building or renovation.

The defendant in *Swaine v Great Northern Railway Co* [1864] dumped refuse next to the claimant's property before moving it on to another property. The claimant's claim in nuisance failed as it was temporary and occasional.

▨ *Grave temporary interference.* The courts will allow claims for temporary nuisance where the interference is grave. So, in *Matania v National Provincial Bank* [1936], the claimant succeeded when a temporary nuisance, in the form of building works carried on by the defendant's independent contractors, prevented the claimant from carrying on his livelihood as a music teacher.

Similarly, in *De Keyser's Royal Hotel v Spicer Bros* [1914], use of a steam pile-driving machine outside the claimant's hotel, causing hotel guests to lose a night's sleep and preventing after-dinner speakers from making themselves heard, also constituted nuisance.

Contrast *De Keyser's Royal Hotel* with *Murdoch v Glacier Metal Co Ltd* [1998], where excess noise from a nearby factory, which exceeded World Health Organisation levels, was not actionable nuisance. The property was in a noisy neighbourhood.

▨ *Single act of the defendant.* Nuisance is usually associated with a continuing state of affairs rather than a single act of the defendant. It was held in *British Celanese Ltd v AH Hunt (Capacitors) Ltd* [1969], though, that an isolated occurrence could constitute nuisance.

In *SCM (UK) Ltd v WJ Whittall & Son Ltd* [1970], it was held that a single escape could constitute nuisance; the nuisance must arise from the condition of the defendant's land. It should be remembered that a single occurrence could constitute a right of action under the rule in *Rylands v Fletcher* [1868].

(4) Malice

Motive is generally irrelevant in tort, as can be seen from *Bradford Corporation v Pickles* [1895], where a bad motive on its own did not create a right of action.

This rule needs qualification in the case of private nuisance, as malice may tip the scales in the claimant's favour and conduct which would not otherwise be actionable becomes unlawful and a nuisance if it has been committed maliciously. In *Christie v Davey* [1893], the defendant lived next door to a music teacher. He objected to the noise and retaliated by banging on the walls, beating trays, etc. The claimant was granted an injunction but the outcome would have been different if the acts had been innocent.

In *Hollywood Silver Fox Farm Ltd v Emmett* [1936], the claimants bred silver foxes. If they are disturbed in the breeding season they eat their young. The defendant fired a gun as near as possible to the breeding pens with the malicious intention of causing damage. The defendant was held liable, although the decision has been criticised on the grounds that the silver foxes were an exceptionally delicate trade. It seems that the element of malice was sufficient to alter the outcome.

(5) Public benefit

It is not a defence in nuisance to say that the activity is being carried on for the public benefit, see *Adams v Ursell* [1913]. Nevertheless, if the activity is being carried out for the good of the community in general then the courts are more likely to find the use of the land to be reasonable.

DEFENDANT'S NEGLIGENCE

The fact that a defendant has acted with all reasonable care does not necessarily mean that the use of the land was reasonable and therefore does not constitute nuisance. On the other hand, want of reasonable care may be strong evidence of a nuisance. It is not reasonable to expect a claimant to endure discomfort which the defendant could have avoided with reasonable care.

Lord Reid in *The Wagon Mound* [1967] said that '. . . negligence in the narrow sense may not be necessary, but fault of some kind is almost always necessary, and generally involves foreseeability'.

As nuisance is a tort which relates to use of land, fault in nuisance is thought to relate to unreasonable use of land. This makes fault in nuisance an altogether more subjective concept in nuisance than in negligence. Nuisance does not use the same concepts for assessing fault as negligence. It does not require the existence of a duty of care before establishing the existence of fault but, confusingly, judges have used the terminology of negligence when discussing nuisance. However, foreseeability that an act of nature will cause nuisance can make use of the land unreasonable, see *Leakey v National Trust* [1980]; *Goldman v Hargrave* [1967].

Nuisance is also distinct from negligence in terms of who has *locus standi* to bring a claim and the remedies available.

Liability has been imposed in public nuisance in the absence of fault: *Tarry v Ashton* [1876]; *Wringe v Cohen* [1939].

WHO CAN SUE?

Nuisance protects those persons who have an interest in the land affected, so only an owner or occupier with an interest in the land can sue.

The claimant in *Khorasandjian v Bush* [1993] succeeded without having a proprietary interest in the land. She was being harassed by a former boyfriend. Most of the harassment took place at her mother's home, in which the claimant had no proprietary interest. Dillon LJ said that the law had to be reconsidered in the light of changed social conditions. He felt that as the mother could have sued, there was no reason to prevent the daughter from suing.

Khorasandjian illustrates an expansionary approach to the tort of nuisance. It was decided at a time when it appeared that it would evolve to protect interests other than land. The case was overruled by *Hunter v Canary Wharf* [1997]. The majority of the House of Lords held that the claimant should establish a right to the land affected in order to sue in private nuisance. This restricts nuisance as a tort designed to protect interests in land.

In cases of harassment such as *Khorasandjian*, the House of Lords suggested that claimants might proceed under different causes of action. The rights of action mentioned were negligence, the rule in *Wilkinson v Downton*, and the Protection from Harassment Act 1997.

The 1997 Act creates civil remedies and criminal offences in respect of 'a course of conduct which amounts to harassment' which the defendant 'knows or ought to know amounts to harassment'. Conduct will be regarded as harassing if a reasonable person in possession of the same information thought that it was harassing.

In *Malone v Laskey* [1907], the wife of a licensee whose enjoyment of the land was interfered with could not sue in nuisance as she did not have a proprietary interest in that land.

WHO CAN BE SUED?

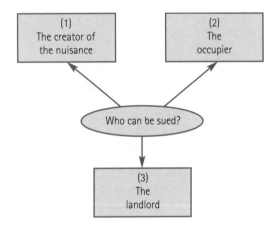

(1) The creator of the nuisance

A person who creates a nuisance by positive conduct may be sued. It is not necessary for the creator of the nuisance to have any interest in the land from which the nuisance emanates.

In the words of Devlin J in *Southport Corporation v Esso* [1954]: 'I can see no reason why ... if the defendant as a licensee or trespasser misuses someone else's land, he should not be liable for a nuisance in the same way as an adjoining occupier would be.' This view is preferable to that of Hurst LJ in *Hussain v Lancaster CC* [1999]. A defendant in trespass need not be a neighbouring landowner, and the same should be true in nuisance.

(2) The occupier

The occupier is the usual defendant in private nuisance. An occupier will be liable for:

- *Persons under his control.* Under the principles of agency and vicarious liability.

- *Independent contractors.* Where nuisance is an inevitable or foreseeable consequence of work undertaken by independent contractors, the occupier cannot avoid liability by employing a contractor, as in *Matania v National Provincial Bank Ltd* [1936].

- *Actions of a predecessor in title.* An occupier who knows or ought reasonably to have known of the existence of a predecessor in title will be liable for continuing the nuisance if he does not abate it. If the nuisance could not reasonably have been discovered, he will not be liable.

  It was held in *St Anne's Well Brewery Co v Roberts* [1928] that if, at the date of a letting, the landlord knows or ought to know of the condition giving rise to the actionable nuisance, he is liable during the tenancy where he does not take from the tenant a covenant to repair.

- *Actions of trespassers.* An occupier is not liable for a nuisance created on his land by a trespasser unless he adopts or continues the nuisance.

  In *Sedleigh-Denfield v O'Callaghan* [1940], the boundary between the appellant's premises and those of the respondents was a hedge and a ditch, both of which belonged to the respondents. Without informing the respondents, a trespasser laid a pipe in the ditch. Some three years later the pipe became blocked and the appellant's garden was flooded. The respondents' servants had cleared the ditch out twice yearly. The appellant claimed damages in nuisance.

  It was held that he would succeed because the respondents knew or ought to have known of the existence of the nuisance and permitted it to continue without taking prompt and efficient action to abate it.

- *Acts of nature.* At common law, it was thought that an occupier had no duty to abate a nuisance that arose on his land from natural causes. The extent of the obligation was to permit his neighbour access to abate the nuisance. The Privy Council in *Goldman v Hargrave* [1967] established that an occupier is under a duty to do what is reasonable in the circumstances to prevent or minimise a known risk of damage to the neighbour's property.

The appellant was the owner/occupier of land next to the respondents. A tree on the appellant's land was struck by lightning and caught fire. The appellant took steps to deal with the burning tree, but subsequently left the fire to burn itself out and took no steps to prevent the fire spreading. The fire later revived and spread, causing extensive damage to the respondents' land. The appellant was held to be liable.

In *Leakey v National Trust* [1980], the defendants owned a hill that was liable to crack and slip. The claimant owned houses at the foot of the hill. After a large fall the claimants asked the defendants to remove the earth and debris from their land, but they refused, saying they were not responsible for what had occurred. The defendants were held liable in nuisance. It was reasonable to prevent or minimise the known risk of damage or injury to one's neighbour or to his property.

In *Bradburn v Lindsay* [1983], it was held that where houses have mutual rights of support, negligently allowing property to fall into dereliction so as to damage the adjoining premises is actionable in negligence as well as in nuisance.

In *Delaware Mansions v City of Westminster* [2001], the House of Lords held that once an occupier became aware of damage to neighbouring land by the roots of trees growing on his land, he would be liable for unreasonably permitting an ongoing nuisance to continue if he failed to stop the of those roots encroachment.

(3) The landlord

A landlord may be liable for a nuisance arising in three types of situation:

(a) Where the landlord authorised the nuisance. In *Sampson v Hodson* [1981], a tiled terrace was built over the claimant's sitting room and bedroom. The noise was excessive and it was held that the landlord was liable in nuisance.

A landlord, who let flats with poor sound insulation to tenants, was not liable in the tort of nuisance to a tenant whose reasonable use and enjoyment of her flat was interfered with by the ordinary use of an adjoining flat by another tenant (*Baxter v Camden London Borough Council (No 2)* [1999]).

It is arguable that a landowner can be liable for repeated acts constituting nuisance committed from its land by those it knew were in occupation, and where no steps were taken to evict them (*Lippiatt v South Gloucestershire City Council* [1999]).

However, all will depend on the exact circumstances, and in *Hussain v Lancaster CC* [1999] the Court of Appeal found that a local authority was not liable for failing to stop acts of criminal damage by council tenants where the harassment did not emanate from 'common parts' of an estate, such as walkways and avenues. In this case, a claim in negligence also failed an application of the test in *Caparo v Dickman* [1990].

(b) Nuisance existed before the date of the letting.

(c) Where the landlord has an obligation or a right to repair.

The law on landlords' liability for nuisance is still developing and there are conflicting lines of authority which can be confusing – see the House of Lords in *Southwark London BC v Mills* [1999].

DEFENCES

PRESCRIPTION
A defendant who has carried on an activity for 20 years may claim a prescriptive right to commit the nuisance. The activity must be an actionable nuisance for the entire 20-year period.

In *Sturges v Bridgman* [1879], a confectioner and a physician lived next door to each other. The confectioner used two large machines and had done so for more than 20 years. The noise and vibrations had been no problem until the physician built a consulting room at the end of his garden. It was held that the confectioner could not rely on the defence of prescription as there was no actionable nuisance until the consulting room had been built.

Statutory authority

If a statute authorises the defendants' activity, the defendants will not be liable for interferences which are inevitable and could not have been avoided by the exercise of reasonable care.

In *Allen v Gulf Oil Refining Ltd* [1981], a statute authorised the defendants to carry out oil refinement works. The claimant complained of noise, smell and vibration. It was held that the defendants had a defence of statutory authority.

It is *not* a defence to plead:

1   That the claimant moved to the nuisance, see *Sturges v Bridgman* [1879].

   In *Miller v Jackson* [1977], cricket had been played on a village ground since 1905. In 1970, houses were built in such a place that cricket balls went into a garden. It was held that there was a nuisance; there was an interference with the reasonable enjoyment of land. It was no defence to say the claimant had brought trouble onto his own head by moving there.

   In *Baxter v Camden LBC (No 2)* [1999], it was held that *Sturges v Bridgman* does not apply where the parties are landlord and tenant. Such cases were decided on the principle 'caveat lessee' ('let the lessee beware') and the lessee was bound to take the premises as he found them.

2   That there is a substantial public benefit.

   In *Adams v Ursell* [1913], the defendant ran a fish and chip shop. The claimant objected to the noise and smells. The defendant tried to argue that the fish and chip shop was of public benefit, but it was held that this was no defence.

3   That the nuisance is the result of the separate actions of several people.

   In *Pride of Derby and Derbyshire Angling Association Ltd v British Celanese Ltd* [1953], pollutant sewage from factories reached a river through the effluent pipe of a local authority from the sewage works. It was held that the local authority was responsible.

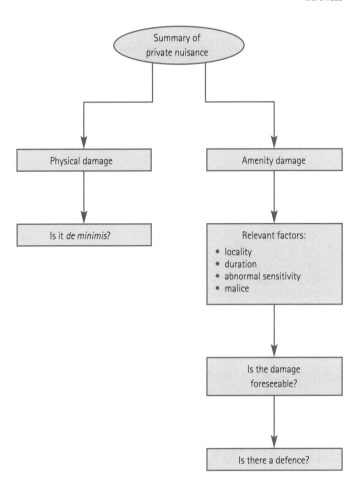

REMEDIES

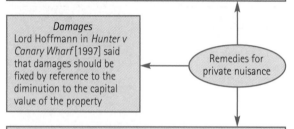

Abatement or self-help

Notice should be given except in an emergency or where it is not necessary to enter the wrongdoer's land

In *Co-operative Wholesale Society Limited v British Railways Board* [1995], it was held that the right to abatement was confined to cases where the security of lives and property required immediate and speedy action, or where such action could be exercised simply without recourse to the expense and inconvenience of legal proceedings in circumstances unlikely to give rise to argument or dispute. Where an application to court could be made, the remedy of self-help was neither appropriate nor desirable

Damages
Lord Hoffmann in *Hunter v Canary Wharf* [1997] said that damages should be fixed by reference to the diminution to the capital value of the property

Remedies for private nuisance

Injunction

An injunction is an equitable and therefore a discretionary remedy

If the nuisance is a continuing one the claimant will be granted an injunction unless:

(a) the injury to the claimant's legal rights is small
(b) and is one capable of being estimated in money
(c) and is one adequately compensated by a small money payment
(d) and it is a case where it would be oppressive to the defendants to grant an injunction

PUBLIC NUISANCE

A public nuisance is a crime as well as a tort. The remedy for a public nuisance is a prosecution or relator action by the Attorney General on behalf of the public. A claimant who suffers particular damage, over and above the damage suffered by the rest of the public, may maintain an action in public nuisance. Public nuisance has been defined as 'an act or omission which materially affects the reasonable comfort of a class of Her Majesty's subjects', *per* Romer LJ in *AG v PYA Quarries Ltd* [1957].

PUBLIC NUISANCE IS MOST IMPORTANT IN RELATION TO HIGHWAYS

What obstructions are actionable?

▨ A temporary or permanent obstruction that is reasonable in amount and duration will not be a nuisance.

In *Russell* [1805], the defendant left wagons standing on the street for several hours at a time for the purpose of loading and unloading and this was held to be a public nuisance.

In *AG v Gastonia Coaches Ltd* [1977], overnight parking of coaches in the street constituted a nuisance.

▨ An obstruction which creates a foreseeable danger will amount to a nuisance.

In *Ware v Garston Haulage Co* [1943], it was held that an unlit vehicle parked at night so as to obstruct the highway may cause a nuisance, although it will depend on the facts.

In *Dymond v Pearce* [1972], the defendant parked a lorry overnight under a lit street lamp without lights. This was regarded as a nuisance, although the claimant did not succeed as the nuisance was not the cause of the claimant's injury.

Premises adjoining the highway

Tarry v Ashton [1876] is an example of public nuisance being capable of amounting to a tort of strict liability. The defendant's lamp projected over the highway. An independent contractor repaired the lamp but it fell on the claimant. The defendant was found liable in the absence of fault.

Similarly, in *Wringe v Cohen* [1939], a wall of the defendants' house, which was let to weekly tenants, collapsed. The defendants, who were liable to keep the house in a good state of repair, did not know that the wall was in a dangerous condition but were nevertheless held to be liable. In *Mint v Good* [1950], again, a wall in front of houses which were let to weekly tenants collapsed, although there was no express agreement between the landlord and tenant as to repair.

The landlord was held to be liable.

DOES THE OCCUPIER HAVE TO BE AWARE OF THE NUISANCE?

In *R v Shorrock* [1993], the defendant let a field on his farm to three persons for a weekend for £2,000. The defendant did not know the purpose for which the field had been let. The field was used for an acid house party lasting 15 hours and attended by between 3,000 and 5,000 people who paid £15 admission each. Many local people complained about the noise and disturbance caused by the party, and the defendant and the organisers were charged with public nuisance.

It was held that it was not necessary to show that the defendant had actual knowledge of the nuisance but merely that he knew or ought to have known the consequences of activities carried out on his land. The defendant ought to have known that there was a real risk that the consequences of the licence would create the nuisance that occurred.

NATURE OF THE LOCALITY

Where there has been planning consent for a development or change of use, the question of the nature of the locality will be determined by reference to the neighbourhood as it is with that development or change of use, not as it was previously.

In *Gillingham BC v Medway (Chatham) Dock Co Ltd* [1992], the claimants had granted planning permission for a naval dockyard to be transformed into a commercial dockyard, with the assurance given to the defendants that they would have unrestricted access to the dockyard and would be consulted before any change of access was made. Access to the dockyard was through a residential district and the claimants sought an injunction to restrain the movement of lorries at night.

It was held that the question of the nature of the locality had to be determined by reference to the nature of the locality after the passing of the planning consents, not as it was previously.

DAMAGE

The claimant must suffer direct and substantial damage to bring an action in public nuisance.

The following have been held to be special damage:

- additional transport costs, caused by an obstruction, see *Rose v Miles* [1815];

- obstructing access to a coffee shop, see *Benjamin v Storr* [1874]; and

- obstructing the view of a procession so that the claimant lost profit on renting a room, see *Campbell v Paddington BC* [1911].

THE RULE IN *RYLANDS v FLETCHER*

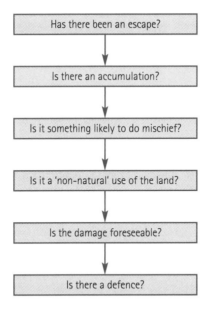

Has there been an escape?

Is there an accumulation?

Is it something likely to do mischief?

Is it a 'non-natural' use of the land?

Is the damage foreseeable?

Is there a defence?

> ❱ RYLANDS v FLETCHER [1868]

Basic facts

The defendant mill owners hired apparently competent contractors to construct a reservoir on their land to store water for use in their mill. The defendants were unaware that disused mine shafts and passages under their land connected with the claimant's mine workings; the claimant's mine was flooded when the reservoir was filled.

Relevance

The defendant was liable for the escape of water from his land because he had made a 'non-natural' use of his land.

The rule in *Rylands v Fletcher* [1868] is a rule of strict liability, that is, it does not require proof of negligence or lack of care, or wrongful intention, on the part of the defendant. Actual damage must be proved, however; it is not a tort that is actionable *per se*.

THE ORIGINAL STATEMENT

The rule was originally formulated by Blackburn J in *Rylands v Fletcher* in the following terms:

The person who for his own purposes brings on his land and collects and keeps there anything likely to do mischief if it escapes, must keep it in at his own peril and, if he does not do so, is *prima facie* answerable for all the damage which is the natural consequence of the escape.

This was approved by the House of Lords, and the condition that there must be a 'non-natural user' was added by Lord Cairns.

Limits of the rule

These may be summarised as follows:

■ There must have been an *escape* of something 'likely to do mischief'.

■ There must have been a *non-natural use* of the land.

THERE MUST BE AN ESCAPE

In *Read v Lyons & Co Ltd* [1947], it was said that escape, for the purposes of applying the proposition in *Rylands v Fletcher*, means 'escape from a place where the defendant has occupation or control over land to a place which is outside his occupation or control', *per* Lord Simon, and 'there must be the escape of something from one man's close to another man's close', *per* Lord Macmillan.

In *Read v Lyons*, the claimant was a munitions worker who was injured by an exploding shell while in the defendant's munitions factory. It was held that there had not been an escape of a dangerous thing, so the defendant could not be liable under *Rylands v Fletcher*.

The claimant must prove not only that there has been an escape, but also that damage is a natural consequence of the escape.

DOES THE CLAIMANT HAVE TO BE AN OCCUPIER?

There is a dispute as to whether or not it is necessary to have an interest in the land in order to maintain a claim under the rule in *Rylands v Fletcher*.

While there are comments in such cases as *Read v Lyons* and *Weller & Foot and Mouth DRI* [1965] which seem to suggest that the claimant must be an occupier or have some interest in the land, other cases adopt a broader view. Lawton J said *obiter* in *British Celanese v AH Hunt* [1969] that the claimant need not be the occupier of adjoining land, or any land. Furthermore, it was held that to use the premises for manufacturing was an ordinary use of the land.

In *Transco v Stockport MBC* [2003], however, the House of Lords approved the categorization of *Rylands v Fletcher* as an offshoot of nuisance. Accordingly, it follows that like nuisance, *Rylands* is a tort to land. Only the landowner can sue, and remedies are available to compensate the reduction in value to land only: *Hunter v Canary Wharf* [1997]. This implicitly overrules a long line of previous authority suggesting that personal injury caused by the escape of dangerous material fell within *Rylands v Fletcher*.

NON-NATURAL USER

This requirement was added by Lord Cairns in the House of Lords in *Rylands v Fletcher* itself. This expression is highly flexible and enables the court to take into account its own interpretation of contemporaneous needs. The way the Privy Council expressed the position in *Rickards v Lothian* [1913] emphasised the flexibility:

> It must be some special use bringing with it increased danger to others and must not merely be the ordinary use of the land or such a use as is proper for the general benefit of the community.

There have, however, been decided cases which have maintained that certain circumstances can confidently be regarded as being outside the sphere of *Rylands v Fletcher*, because the courts have held that the land is being naturally used. For example:

■ lighting of a fire in a fireplace, see *Sochacki v Sas* [1947];

■ storing metal foil strips in a factory, see *British Celanese v AH Hunt* [1969].

In deciding what constitutes a natural use, Lord Porter in *Read v Lyons* said:

> . . . each seems to be a question of fact subject to a ruling by the judge as to whether . . . the particular use can be non-natural and in deciding this question I think that all the circumstances of the time and place and practice of mankind must be taken into consideration, so what might be regarded as . . . non-natural may vary according to the circumstances.

For example, storage of motor parts and engines in *Mason v Levy Auto Parts* [1967] was not a natural use having regard to the large quantities of combustible material, manner of storage and character of the neighbourhood.

Non-natural use is a flexible concept and will vary according to time and context. For example, in *Perry v Kendricks Transport* [1956], the Court of Appeal found itself bound by the decision of *Musgrove v Pandelis* [1919] in holding that a full tank of petrol was a non-natural use of the land. Some commentators maintain that this would not be applied today.

Storage of chemicals for industrial use in large quantities was held to be a non-natural use in *Cambridge Water Co Ltd v Eastern Counties Leather plc* [1994].

In *Ellison v Ministry of Defence* [1997], rainwater which accumulated naturally on an airfield and was not artificially kept there was held to be a natural use of the land. Consequently, it fell outside the rule in *Rylands v Fletcher*.

In *Transco v Stockport MBC* [2003] the House of Lords stressed that the the thing accumulated must pose a very high risk of damage, should it escape. Furthermore, it must be something considered highly unusual, given the place and time of the escape. Accordingly, the supply of water to a block of flats via a high-pressure pipe was held not to be a 'non-natural use' and the defendant council was not liable.

'BRINGS ONTO HIS LAND AND KEEPS THERE'

The thing may or may not be something which in its nature is capable of being there naturally. What matters is whether the particular thing has in fact been accumulated there. *Rylands v Fletcher* applies only to things artificially brought or kept upon the defendant's land.

There is no liability for things naturally on the land, such as the spread of this-tles from ploughed land in *Giles v Walker* [1890], or rocks falling from a natural outcrop in *Pontardawe Rural District Council v Moore Gwyn* [1929].

More recently, flooding by rainwater was held to be something which occurred naturally on the land and was not an accumulation, in *Ellison v Ministry of Defence* [1997].

These cases can be contrasted with *Crowhurst v Amersham Burial Board* [1878], where yew trees planted close to railings spread onto an adjoining meadow on which the claimant pastured his horse, which was poisoned and died as a result of eating yew leaves. The defendant was liable; although the yew trees were capable of being there naturally, the defendant had planted the trees and therefore they constituted an accumulation.

'ANYTHING LIKELY TO DO MISCHIEF IF IT ESCAPES'

This is a question of fact in each case. However, things which have been held to be within the rule include electricity, gas which was likely to pollute water supplies, explosives, fumes and water.

A very broad view can be taken. In *AG v Corke* [1933], it was held that the owner of land who allowed caravan dwellers to live on it was answerable for the inter-ference they caused on adjoining land, on the basis that they were 'things likely to do mischief'.

DEFENCES

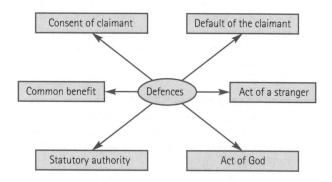

Consent of the claimant

If the claimant has permitted the accumulation of the thing which escapes, he cannot sue. Implied consent, such as common benefit, is also a defence.

Common benefit

If the accumulation benefits both the claimant and the defendant, this is an important element in deciding whether the claimant is deemed to have consented.

In *Carstairs v Taylor* [1871], rainwater which had been collected on the roof of a block of flats for the benefit of several occupants meant that the landlord was not liable when the water escaped as it had been accumulated for a common benefit. In *Peters v Prince of Wales Theatre* [1942], a fire extinguisher which exploded, damaging part of the building occupied by the claimants, was also held to have been accumulated for a common benefit.

Act of a stranger

It is a defence that the escape was caused by the unforeseeable act of a stranger over whom the defendant has no control.

In *Rickards v Lothian* [1913], someone deliberately blocked a basin in the defendant's premises and turned the taps on, flooding the claimant's premises below. In *Perry v Kendricks Transport* [1956], the claimant was injured by an explosion caused by a boy trespasser who threw a lighted match into a petrol tank. The Court of Appeal held that the defendants were not liable as they had no control over trespassers and had not been negligent.

Foreseeable act of a stranger. The defendant in *Hale v Jennings* [1938] ought reasonably to have foreseen the act of a third party and had enough control over the premises to prevent the escape.

Act of God

If an escape is caused, through natural causes and without human intervention, in 'circumstances which no human foresight can provide against and of which human prudence is not bound to recognise the possibility' (*Tennent v Earl of Glasgow* [1864]), then there is said to be the defence of Act of God.

In *Nichols v Marsland* [1876], the defence succeeded where a violent thunderstorm caused flooding.

The case was put into proper perspective by the House of Lords in *Greenock Corporation v Caledonian Railway Company* [1917], where an extraordinary and unprecedented rainfall was held in similar circumstances not to be an Act of God. The explanation of *Nichols v Marsland* [1876] was that there the jury found that no reasonable person could have anticipated the storm and the court would not disturb a finding of fact.

Earthquakes and tornadoes may sometimes be Acts of God but few other phenomena seem likely to be within the scope of *Rylands v Fletcher.*

Statutory authority

Sometimes, public bodies storing water, gas, electricity and the like are by statute exempted from liability so long as they have taken reasonable care. It is a question of statutory interpretation whether and, if so, to what extent, liability under *Rylands v Fletcher* is excluded.

Liability was excluded in *Green v Chelsea Waterworks Co* [1894] when, without negligence on the defendants' part, their water main exploded and flooded the claimant's premises.

This can be compared to *Charing Cross Electric Co v London Hydraulic Power Co* [1914], where the defendants were liable when their hydraulic main burst even though there was no question of negligence on their part, as the statute did not exempt them from liability.

Default of the claimant

The defendant is not liable where damage is caused by the claimant's act or default. If the claimant is partially responsible then the Law Reform (Contributory Negligence) Act 1945 will apply.

In *Ponting v Noakes* [1894], the defendant's colt reached onto the defendant's land and ate some branches of a yew tree and died. The action did not succeed as the animal's death was due to its wrongful intrusion.

Where the damage is attributable to the extra sensitivity of the claimant's property then there is no liability, see *Eastern and South African Telegraph Co Ltd v Cape Town Tramways Co Ltd* [1902].

REMOTENESS OF DAMAGE

Negligence	Private Nuisance	*Rylands v Fletcher*
Reasonable foreseeability: *The Wagon Mound (No 1)* [1961] but also competing test of direct consequences: *Re Polemis* [1921]; *Page v Smith* [1994]	Reasonable foreseeability: *The Wagon Mound (No 2)* [1967]	Reasonable foreseeability: *Cambridge Water v Eastern Counties Leather* [1994]

FUTURE OF STRICT LIABILITY FOR HAZARDOUS ACTIVITIES

The scope of the rule in *Rylands v Fletcher* has been cut down considerably by the requirements that there be a non-natural use and the exclusion of 'ordinary' industrial processes: *British Celanese v AH Hunt* [1969].

The defences, particularly act of a stranger and statutory authority, turn a tort of strict liability into an inquisition on the defendant's culpability.

The Pearson Commission recommended a statutory scheme of strict liability for personal injuries resulting from exceptional risks. Under the scheme, strict liability would be imposed in two circumstances:

■ those which, due to unusually hazardous activities, require close, careful supervision; and

▨ those which, although normally safe, are likely to cause serious and extensive casualties if they do go wrong.

Contributory negligence and voluntary assumption of the risk would be general defences, but statutory authority and act of a third party would not. The fact that the claimant was a trespasser would not be a general defence but could be introduced as a defence to a specific type of exceptional risk when making the statutory instrument.

According to Lord Goff in *Cambridge Water Co Ltd v Eastern Counties Leather plc* [1994], the turning point (which meant that *Rylands* could never develop into a general tort of liability for dangerous things) was *Read v Lyons* [1947] – the requirement of an escape makes no sense in such a general tort, but only in a tort between landowners. As pointed out above, the strictness of *Rylands v Fletcher* is considerably attenuated by the non-natural user doctrine, and the various defences. Accordingly, the High Court of Australia in *Burnie Port Authority v General Jones Pty Ltd* [1996] declared that there was no such thing as a separate tort of *Rylands v Fletcher* – it was completely subsumed within the modern tort of negligence. In *Transco v Stockport MBC* [2003], the House of Lords refused to take such a step in England, stating that it is for Parliament alone to abolish such a well-established doctrine. However, the judges recognised that the tort is of very minor importance in practice – Lord Hoffmann claimed that there has been no successful action based solely on *Rylands v Fletcher* since the Second World War.

THE HUMAN RIGHTS ACT 1998

The European Convention on Human Rights, incorporated into domestic law by the Human Rights Act (HRA) 1998, protects the right to respect for the home (Art 8) and the right to peaceful enjoyment of possessions (First Protocol, Art 1). It may be that an expansion of liability for interference with land will result.

In *Marcic v Thames Water Utilities*, the defendants declined to make the expensive improvements to their drainage systems which were necessary to prevent flooding to the claimant's house. The trial judge (2001) held that there was no liability for failing to exercise such statutory powers (see Chapter 1), but that the flooding had breached the claimant's rights under Art 8 and the defendants had failed to justify that interference by a pressing social need. The

Court of Appeal (2002) held that there was liability at common law, and no need to rule on the HRA claim. The court did suggest, *obiter*, that routine compensation on a no fault basis might be necessary where the activities of public bodies infringe the Convention rights of a minority of the community (cf Land Compensation Act 1973). The House of Lords (2003) restored the trial judge's conclusion that there was no liability on ordinary principles of nuisance.

A statutory sewerage undertaker could not be equated to a normal landowner for the purposes of the *Leakey v National Trust* principle, see p 91; instead, the Water Industry Act 1991 provided a scheme of remedies (enforcement orders issued by the Director General of Water Services). Furthermore, for the purposes of the HRA claim, it could not be said that this statutory scheme struck the wrong balance between the rights of homeowners and the cost to the public of making such improvements. As elsewhere, there is a constitutional imperative that the courts defer to the legislature when such judgments are to be made.

In *McKenna v British Aluminium* [2002], the High Court ruled that a prospective claimant under *Rylands v Fletcher* must have a proprietary interest in the land affected (following *Read v Lyons*, see above). However, the court refused to strike out the claims, holding that it was arguable that the HRA could give rise to an extension of the common law rule. These cases are certainly not the final word but show that the HRA will be a major source of innovation in this area of the law – and indeed, in tort law more generally – in the years to come.

You should now be confident that you would be able to tick all of the boxes on the checklist at the beginning of this chapter. To check your knowledge of Torts relating to land why not visit the companion website and take the Multiple Choice Question test. Check your understanding of the terms and vocabulary used in this chapter with the flashcard glossary.

Defamation and privacy

4

DEFAMATION

The tort of defamation protects individuals from losing their reputation by prohibiting publication of information likely to attract negative attention. It is often encountered in high-profile media cases involving public figures, although it can, of course, be used by anyone. That said, there is no public funding for defamation actions, so it favours those who can afford to pay to protect their reputation. It attempts to strike a balance between the right to privacy (Article 8 ECHR) and the right to freedom of expression (Article 10 ECHR).

There are two forms of defamantion: **slander and libel**

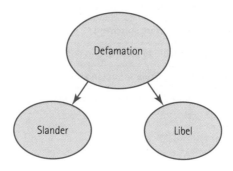

SLANDER AND LIBEL

Both slander and libel relate to statements that have been made, but differ in the way in which the statement is publicised. There are also differences in what must be established by the claimant in order for liability to arise.

Slander	Libel
Statement must be in non-permanent form (words or gestures)	Statement must be written or broadcasted
Claimant must establish loss or harm that is financially quantifiable (but there are exceptions)	Actionable *per se*. It does not matter whether the claimant has suffered harm

The exceptions to the requirement for the claimant to show financially-quantifiable loss or harm in cases of slander relate to the nature of the slanderous statement and are as follows:

▓ That the claimant has committed a serious criminal offence

▓ That the claimant is unfit, dishonest or incompetent with regard to their trade or profession

▓ That the claimant has a contagious or infectious disease

▓ That the claimant is sexually promiscuous or adulterous (only applies to female claimants)

Both parties must be alive and claims must be commenced within 12 months of the statement being made (Limitation Act 1980, s 4A). If the case is not too complex, there is a right to trial by jury (Superior Courts Act 1981, s 69) although this can be avoided provided that both parties agree to do so. Jury trials for defamation consist of two stages – first, the judge considers whether the statements are capable of being defamatory and then the jury decides, if so, whether the statements do, in fact, defame the claimant. Only one other person has to read or hear the statement for liability to arise: there is no requirement for any sort of mass publication.

DEFAMATORY STATEMENTS
A defamatory statement is one which is designed to 'lower the claimant in the estimation of right thinking members of society' (*Sim v Stretch* [1936]).

▶ BYRNE v DEANE (1937)

Basic facts
The defendants owned a golf club where illegal gambling machines were kept. Someone told the police and they were removed. Shortly after a piece of paper appeared on one of the walls saying but 'he who gave the game away, may he byrnn in hell and rue the day'.

Relevance
No right-thinking member of society would think less of a person for reporting illegal activity to the police so the words could not be defamatory. However, the case succeeded as the verse also implied disloyalty to the golf club, which would lower their standing in the eyes of right-thinking members of society.

Examples of defamatory statements include

■ An actor who was described as hideously ugly: *Berkoff v Birchill* [1996]

■ An actor was said to be a homosexual: *Donovan v The Face* [1992]

■ A married woman was 'living in sin': *Cassidy v Daily Mirror Newspapers Ltd* [1929]

Both parties must be alive and claims must be commenced within 12 months of the statement being made (Limitation Act 1980, s 4A). If the case is not too complex, there is a right to trial by jury (Superior Courts Act 1981).

The claimant must also show that the defamation refers to them as an individual – this is usually obvious from the nature of the statement, but the courts have also held that a claim may be made if a reasonable person would think that the statement referred to the claimant (*Newstead v London Express Newspaper Ltd* [1940]) even if this implication was not intended to be made or the person making the statement actually intended to refer to someone else (*Morgan v Oldhams Press* [1971]).

DEFENCES TO DEFAMATION

There are several defences available to an action in defamation.

Privilege refers to circumstances in which individuals are able to express their views without fear of legal action. Therefore, the interests of freedom of expression take priority over the rights of the individual in protecting their reputation.

Absolute privilege	Qualified privilege
Statements made during judicial and Parliamentary proceedings where there is an interest in ensuring that parties are able to speak freely without fear of legal proceedings. Any statements covered by absolute privilege cannot be relied upon in legal proceedings and so cannot be used as the basis for a defamation claim.	Situations in which there is a duty to disclose information even if it is unfavourable to the claimant, such as an employment reference. These are only actionable if the defendant acted with malice.

▶ REYNOLDS v TIMES NEWSPAPERS (2001)

Basic facts

The Times had published an article stating Reynolds, the former Irish Prime Minister, had misled the Irish Parliament. This article was subsequently published in the UK but did not include the explanation that Reynolds had given for the events, which had been printed in the original article. Reynolds brought an action for defamation. The House of Lords had to decide whether qualified privilege should be extended to cover the mass media.

Relevance

The House of Lords provided a list of 10 criteria against which attempts to use the *Reynolds* defence should be judged. As Lord Nicholls stated:

> The elasticity of the common law principle enables interference with freedom of speech to be confined to what is necessary in the circumstances of the case. This elasticity enables the court to give appropriate weight, in today's conditions, to the importance of freedom of expression by the media on all matters of public concern. Depending on the circumstances, the matters to be taken into account include the following. The comments are illustrative only.

(1) The seriousness of the allegation. The more serious the charge, the more the public is misinformed and the individual harmed, if the allegation is not true.

(2) The nature of the information, and the extent to which the subject-matter is a matter of public concern.

(3) The source of the information. Some informants have no direct knowledge of the events. Some have their own axes to grind, or are being paid for their stories.

(4) The steps taken to verify the information.

(5) The status of the information. The allegation may have already been the subject of an investigation which commands respect.

(6) The urgency of the matter. News is often a perishable commodity.

(7) Whether comment was sought from the plaintiff. He may have information others do not possess or have not disclosed. An approach to the plaintiff will not always be necessary.

(8) Whether the article contained the gist of the plaintiff's side of the story.

(9) The tone of the article. A newspaper can raise queries or call for an investigation. It need not adopt allegations as statements of fact.

(10) The circumstances of the publication, including the timing.

This list is not exhaustive. The weight to be given to these and any other relevant factors will vary from case to case. Any disputes of primary fact will be a matter for the jury, if there is one. The decision on whether, having regard to the admitted or proved facts, the publication was subject to qualified privilege is a matter for the judge. This is the established practice and seems sound. A balancing operation is better carried out by a judge in a reasoned judgment than by a jury. Over time, a valuable corpus of case law will be built up.

This defence has been subsequently considered and applied by the courts in *Jameel (Mohammed) v Wall Street Journal Europe Sprl (No. 3)* [2007] and *Roberts v Gable* [2008]. In *Seaga v Harper* [2009] the Privy Council considered that the defence extends to publication of any public interest material in whatever medium.

Consent to publication removes the right to bring an action in defamation.

True statements cannot be defamatory; this is also so if there are minor peripheral inaccuracies in the otherwise true statement (Defamation Act 1952, s 5)

Fair comment applies to critical comment based upon true facts. It generally involves media comments about matters of public interest and the defence regards that the person making the comment must believe it to be based on a true statement and must not be acting maliciously. In *Lowe v Associated Newspapers* [2007] the Divisional Court held that the ultimate test of a defence of fair comment was the objective one of whether someone could have expressed the commentator's defamatory opinion upon the facts known to the commentator, at least in general terms, and upon which he was purporting to comment. See also *British Chiropractic Association v Singh* [2010] in which the Court of Appeal stated that 'fair comment' is a misleading term and suggested that 'honest opinion' would be preferable.

In *Spiller v Joseph* [2011], the Supreme Court commented on the reform of fair comment and libel laws more generally such as widening the scope of the defence of 'honest comment' by removing the public interest requirement. Lord Phillips also commented that it might be preferable for juries to be removed from defamation trials, given that defamation cases often involve issues too complex for juries.

Innocent publication of statements cannot be defamatory: if a person (who is not author, editor, or publisher) reproduces material that they believe to be true after taking reasonable care in publication (Defamation Act 1952, s 1). This includes the passive role played by internet service providers (*Bunt v Tilley* [2007])

Although not strictly speaking a defence, section 2 of the Defamation Act 1996 allows publishers to avoid liability if they make a suitable correction and apology, published in a reasonable manner and pay compensation to the claimant.

REMEDIES FOR DEFAMATION
The most common remedy for a successful defamation claim is an award of **damages**, the level of which is determined by the jury. The Courts and Legal Services Act 1990 allows for the amount of damages to be reassessed by the Court of Appeal if the award by the jury is inappropriate, such as the reduction from £250,000 to £110,000 in *Rantzen v Mirror Group Newspapers* [1994].

Injunctions in defamation cases can take two forms (*Bonnard v Perryman* [1891]):

- an injunction can be sought after a successful defamation claim if the claimant can establish that there is a real risk of repetition of the publication.

- an interlocutory injunction can be obtained to prevent publication of defamatory material if the claimant is aware that this is likely;

MISUSE OF PRIVATE INFORMATION

Defamation focuses attention on the debate about the appropriate balance between an individual's right to privacy and the conflicting right to freedom of expression.

There is no tort of breach of privacy. However, the Human Rights Act 1998, which requires public bodies to act compatibly with Convention rights, also expressly binds the courts. Therefore, if a claim is made that a private body has acted in breach of Convention rights, then the court must comply with its obligation under the HRA and ensure that it acts compatibly with Convention rights.

The HRA therefore allows individuals to seek redress in the domestic courts for breaches of their Convention rights committed by other private bodies. The courts have, through this process, developed the law of confidence to provide some protection against breaches of privacy committed by private bodies.

In *Campbell v Mirror Group Newspapers* [2004], the model Naomi Campbell sued the *Daily Mirror* newspaper when it published photographs of her leaving a meeting of Narcotics Anonymous. The House of Lords stated that tort of breach of confidence had developed such that there now was a tort that would be better termed as '**misuse of private information**'.

Misuse of private information is based on the obligation of confidence which can arise out of particular relationships. The obligation may be imposed by an express or implied term in a contract or independently of any contract on the basis of the independent principle of confidence. There may be no financial detriment where the breach of confidence involves no more than an invasion of personal privacy.

Therefore, if information in respect of which the claimant had a 'reasonable expectation of privacy' is published, then an action for misuse of private information may be possible. The question of whether or not the information will be considered information in respect of which there is a 'reasonable expectation of privacy' is a broad one, which takes account of all the circumstances of the case, including:

■ the particular attributes of the claimant, such as whether they are normally in the public eye, or whether they are a child or an adult (children have a greater expectation of privacy),

- the nature of the activity in which the claimant was engaged

- the place at which it was happening,

- the nature and purpose of the intrusion

- the absence of consent and whether it was known or could be inferred,

- the effect on the claimant of the publication,

- the circumstances in which and the purposes for which the information came into the hands of the publisher.

If the court considers that the claimant did have a reasonable expectation of privacy, then the court will need to consider the right to respect for private life, which is protected by Article 8. If there is an infringement of Article 8 rights, publication will be a misuse of personal information. This means that the court will be able to order an injunction prohibiting the publication, or to award damages to compensate for the breach of privacy.

For example, in *A v B plc* [2003], a professional footballer sought to prevent publication of 'kiss and tell' revelations on the basis that they interfered with his right to a private life. The story in this case was true so the claimant could not rely on defamation to prevent publication. The Court of Appeal considered that scurrilous stories of casual sexual encounters deserved little protection so the right of the other party involved and the newspaper to freedom of expression should prevail. The Court of Appeal was clear that the newspapers should be free to publish without constraint provided they were within the Press Complaints Commission Code.

You should now be confident that you would be able to tick all of the boxes on the checklist at the beginning of this chapter. To check your knowledge of Defamation and privacy why not visit the companion website and take the Multiple Choice Question test. Check your understanding of the terms and vocabulary used in this chapter with the flashcard glossary?

5

General defences

What is the effect of a finding of contributory negligence?	
Can it ever reduce a damages award by 100 per cent?	
Is consent/*volenti non fit injuria* a complete defence?	
Does it matter if the claimant was involved in an illegal or immoral act?	
How does the Limitation Act 1980 limit actions?	

So far, we have been primarily concerned with what a claimant has to prove in order to establish the existence of a tort.

This is a convenient point to consider certain defences that may be raised by the defendant who, while admitting the behaviour complained of (which would otherwise constitute a tort), then seeks to adduce in evidence additional facts which will excuse what he has done. So, the burden of proving the facts to establish the defence rests on the defendant.

CONTRIBUTORY NEGLIGENCE

POSITION AT COMMON LAW

At common law, it was a complete defence if the defendant proved that the claimant had been guilty of contributory negligence. In *Butterfield v Forrester* [1809], the defendant negligently left a pole lying across the road. The claimant was injured when he collided with the pole when riding along the road. Although the defendant had been negligent, he escaped liability as the claimant would have avoided the accident if he had not been riding so fast.

This resulted in undue hardship to the claimant and so, to mitigate its harshness, the courts developed the rule of 'last opportunity', which meant that whoever was negligent last in time was treated as the sole cause of the damage on the basis that they had been the last one to have the opportunity to avoid the accident. The rule was applied in *Davies v Mann* [1842]. The claimant tied the feet of his donkey and negligently left him on the highway. The defendant, who was driving his wagon faster than necessary, collided with the donkey, which was killed. The defendant was liable. If he had been driving at the correct speed he would have avoided the donkey, so he had the last opportunity to avoid the accident.

A rule of 'constructive last opportunity' was created in *British Columbia Electric Railway Co Ltd v Loach* [1916].

LAW REFORM (CONTRIBUTORY NEGLIGENCE) ACT 1945

This linear sequential approach to liability was most difficult to apply in cases where events occurred simultaneously.

The problems led to the Law Reform (Contributory Negligence) Act 1945, which introduced apportionment of damages for accidents occurring on land. It is now possible for the courts to reduce the damages awarded against the defendant to the extent to which the claimant was contributorily negligent.

▶ PITTS v HUNT [1991]

Basic facts

After consuming large quantities of alcohol the claimant encouraged the defendant to drive his motorbike in a reckless and dangerous way. The defendant had never passed a test and was uninsured. The defendant was killed and the claimant (who had been riding pillion) was badly injured in the inevitable accident.

Relevance

Damages can never be reduced by 100 per cent, and therefore contributory negligence can only be a partial defence.

Scope of the Law Reform (Contributory Negligence) Act 1945

Under s 4 of the Act, fault means 'negligence, breach of statutory duty or other act or omission which gives rise to liability in tort'. So the Act applies to nuisance and *Rylands v Fletcher* as well as to negligence.

However, in *Standard Chartered Bank v Pakistan Shipping* [2002], it was held that contributory negligence is not available as a defence in the tort of deceit (or fraudulent misstatement).

Establishing contributory negligence

In order to establish and prove contributory negligence, the defendant must plead and prove:

- that the claimant's injury results from the risk to which the claimant's negligence exposed him;

- that the claimant's negligence contributed to his injury;

- that there was fault or negligence on the part of the claimant.

Claimant's negligence contributed to his injury

It is not necessary to show that the claimant owes the defendant a duty of care, merely that the claimant has contributed to the injury and not necessarily the cause of the accident. So, in *O'Connell v Jackson* [1971], there was a 15 per cent reduction in the damages awarded to a motorcyclist because of his failure to wear a crash helmet. Similarly, in *Froom v Butcher* [1975], there was a 25 per cent reduction to a driver for failure to wear a seatbelt, as the injury could have been completely avoided by wearing the seatbelt; but if wearing a seatbelt would have reduced the severity of the injuries, then damages would have been reduced by 15 per cent.

Other examples of a claimant having contributed to the injury include the failure of a motorcyclist to fasten the chin strap of a crash helmet: *Capps v Miller* [1989]; accepting a lift in a car knowing that the driver was drunk: *Owens v Brimmell* [1976], although the burden was on the defendant to show that the claimant knew that the defendant was unfit to drive: *Limbrick v French* [1993]; asking a much younger, inexperienced driver to drive a car when the driver had never driven a powerful, automatic car before: *Donelan v Donelan* [1993]; and crossing a pelican crossing when the pedestrian light was red: *Fitzgerald v Lane* [1989]. In *Commissioner of Police for the Metropolis v Reeves* [1999], the House of Lords held that a prisoner who hanged himself in police custody had been contributorily negligent in relation to his own death. In *Badger v Ministry of Defence* [2005] the damages awarded against an employer for negligently exposing an employee to asbestos fibres which led to the development of lung cancer were reduced by 20 per cent because the employee was contributorily negligent for failing to stop smoking once health warnings were put on cigarette packets.

Claimant's injury results from the risk to which he exposed himself

In *Jones v Livox Quarries Ltd* [1952], the claimant was riding on the back of the defendant's truck contrary to instructions. A vehicle collided with the back of the truck, injuring the claimant. He argued, unsuccessfully, that he had exposed himself to the risk of falling off, not to a collision.

THE STANDARD OF CARE

This is the same standard of care as applies in negligence:

> A person is guilty of contributory negligence if he ought reasonably to have foreseen that, if he did not act as a reasonable, prudent man, he might hurt himself and in his reckonings he must take into account the possibility of others being careless (*per* Denning LJ in *Jones v Livox Quarries*).

In practice, though, the courts seem to demand less of claimants than of defendants.

A look at some particular instances:

(1) Children

Lord Denning MR in *Gough v Thorne* [1966] said that a very young child could not be contributorily negligent.

However, the general test seems to be: what degree of care can an infant of a particular age reasonably be expected to take for his own safety (*Yachuk v Oliver Blais Co Ltd* [1949])? Consequently, a 12-year-old girl was contributorily negligent in *Armstrong v Cotterell* [1993], as a child of that age is expected to know the basic elements of the Highway Code.

In *J v West* All England Official Transcripts 12 July [1999], the Court of Appeal held that a nine-year-old, who had jumped off a kerb into the path of a car to avoid being hit by a friend, was not contributorily negligent.

It was held in *Oliver v Birmingham and Midland Omnibus Co Ltd* [1933] that, where a child is under the control of an adult, negligence on the part of the adult is not imputed to the child.

(2) Accidents at work

The purpose of such statutory regulations as the Factories Acts and those made under the Health and Safety at Work etc Act 1974 is to ensure safety standards in workplaces and to protect workers from their own carelessness.

This being the purpose behind such regulations, in order to ensure that their purpose is not defeated by finding contributory negligence, the courts tend to be less willing to make a finding of contributory negligence in these cases. See *Caswell v Powell Duffryn Associated Collieries Ltd* [1939].

This does not mean that a workman can never be guilty of contributory negligence. In *Jayes v IMI (Kynoch) Ltd* [1984], a workman who put his hand into a piece of moving machinery had his damages reduced by 100 per cent, even though the employer was in breach of his statutory duty to fence the machinery. It should be noted that this case was heard prior to *Pitts v Hunt* [1991] and damages can now never be reduced by 100 per cent.

(3) Emergency

An emergency is a special situation in which a person's reactions may with hindsight be regarded as negligent. The law takes account of this, and provided the claimant has acted reasonably he will not be held to have been contributorily negligent. See *Jones v Boyce* [1816].

CONSENT/*VOLENTI NON FIT INJURIA*

There is considerable confusion between these two concepts. Consent is used to describe the defence that may be used when sued for committing an intentional tort.

Volenti non fit injuria is the appropriate term where the claimant alleges negligence/strict liability tort, that is, an unintentional tort, and the defendant asserts the claimant's voluntary assumption of the risk involved.

The general principles applying to both concepts are the same, but it is important to bear in mind the stature of the tort concerned.

The defence of consent was found to be available to a defendant who clamped the claimant's car in *Arthur v Anker* [1996]. However, certain conditions had to be satisfied before the defence would arise. There would have to be a notice that a vehicle parked without lawful authority would be clamped and released on payment of a fee. The release fee would have to be reasonable. The vehicle would have to be released without delay, once the owner had offered to pay, and there would have to be means by which the owner could communicate his offer of payment.

In *Vine v Waltham Forest London Borough Council* [2000], the claimant's car was clamped when she had to pull off the highway suddenly to vomit. There was a warning notice as required in *Arthur*, but she had not seen it owing to her illness. The Court of Appeal held that she could not, therefore, have consented to the clamping – it refused to apply an objective test to her consent (although the possibility was raised that one who had seen a notice but not read it might yet be bound by its terms).

MERE KNOWLEDGE DOES NOT IMPLY CONSENT

In the case of *Smith v Baker & Sons* [1891], the claimant was an employee of the defendants and was employed in drilling holes in rock cutting. He was aware of the danger of a crane continually swinging over his head. A stone fell out of the crane and injured him. He brought an action in negligence and *volenti non fit injuria* was pleaded.

It was held that mere knowledge of the risk was not enough, it had to be shown that the claimant had consented to the particular thing being done which would involve the risk and consented to take that risk upon himself.

The question in *Dann v Hamilton* [1939] was whether a claimant who accepted a lift from a drunk driver who was obviously inebriated could be taken to have assumed the risk of injury. It was held that *volenti* did not apply, unless the drunkenness was so extreme and so glaring that accepting a lift was equivalent to 'walking on the edge of an unfenced cliff'.

Under s 149 of the Road Traffic Act 1988, defendants are prevented from relying on the *volenti* defence where a passenger sues a driver in circumstances where, under the Act, insurance is compulsory.

However, it may apply where there is no requirement of compulsory insurance under the Act, for example, an aeroplane.

> ▶ **MORRIS v MURRAY [1991]**
>
> Basic facts
> After a heavy drinking session two men decided to take a light aircraft for a flight. The defendant pilot was killed and the claimant badly injured in a crash not long after take off.
>
> Relevance
> The defence successfully argued that the pilot was so obviously and extremely drunk that the claimant was *volens* to the risk.

TO BE EFFECTIVE, CONSENT MUST BE FREELY GIVEN

Normally, as already shown in *Smith v Baker & Sons*, an employee will rarely be held to be *volens*, but there are exceptional cases, such as *ICI v Shatwell* [1964]. The claimant and his brother disregarded the instructions of their employer, and were also in breach of statutory safety regulations, when they chose to test certain detonators without taking the necessary precautions. The claimant was injured in the subsequent explosion. The claimant's action in both negligence and breach of statutory duty failed because of *volenti non fit injuria*. This is an unusual case, however, and *volenti* will not normally arise out of an employee's ordinary duties.

RESCUE CASES

The law is reluctant to apply *volenti* to rescue situations, because to do so would negative the duty of care owed to the claimant.

In *Haynes v Harwood* [1935], a two-horse van was left unattended in the street. A boy threw a stone and the horses ran off, endangering a woman and children. A policeman intercepted and stopped the horses and was injured. It was held that the *volenti* defence did not apply. *Volenti* will apply where there is no real risk of danger and there is not a genuine emergency, see *Cutler v United Dairies (London) Ltd* [1933].

SPORTING EVENTS

In *Smoldon v Whitworth* [1996], a young rugby player sued the referee in negligence for failing to control the scrum properly. The claimant suffered a broken back when the scrum collapsed. It was held that the player had consented to the ordinary incidents of the game. He could not be said to have consented to the breach of duty of an official whose job was to enforce the rules.

In *McCord v Swansea City AFC* [1997], it was held that recklessness was not required to be shown after a clear foul which was outside the laws of the game as there is no *volens* to such acts.

ILLEGAL ACTS

A person who is engaged in an illegal act at the time he is injured may be precluded from a civil claim by the maxim *ex turpi causa non oritur actio* ('no action can arise from a base cause').

A distinction was made by Asquith LJ in *National Coal Board v England* [1954] between two different types of situation:

- the case of two burglars on their way to commit a burglary, and while proceeding one picks the other's pocket; and

- where they have agreed to open a safe by means of high explosive and one negligently handles the explosive charge, injuring the other.

In the first situation, Asquith LJ thought that there would be liability in tort, but not in the second. The idea being that where the illegality is incidental to the cause of action in tort then recovery in tort may still be allowed.

It was held in *Ashton v Turner* [1980] that one participant in a burglary could not succeed against his fellow participant who crashed the car while driving away at high speed from the scene of the crime.

In the case of *Pitts v Hunt* [1991], the claimant was a pillion passenger on a motorcycle. Both the claimant and the defendant who was riding the motorcycle were drunk. The claimant also knew that the defendant was unlicensed and uninsured. The defendant carelessly crashed the motorcycle, killing himself and injuring the claimant. Due to s 149 of the Road Traffic Act 1988, the defence of *volenti* did not apply. Nevertheless, the claimant was found to be *ex turpi*. The majority of the Court of Appeal held that because of the joint illegal activity it was impossible to determine the standard of care.

Most cases have not followed this standard of care test but have, instead, used a test based on whether it would be an affront to public conscience to compensate the claimant.

However, this 'public conscience' test was disapproved by the House of Lords in *Tinsley v Milligan* [1993], where it was said that to base liability on such an 'imponderable factor' as affront to the public conscience would bestow an unacceptably wide discretion upon the courts. In *Vellino v Chief Constable of Greater Manchester* [2001], Sedley LJ said that if judges had to take into account public opinion this would mean, in reality, the views of 'some sections of the media', and this would amount to 'the surrender of judicial independence'.

In *Revill v Newbery* [1996], it was held that the rule did not apply in a claim for personal injuries where the claimant was a trespasser engaged in criminal activities and the defendant had shot the claimant. The defendant was found to have acted negligently, and to have denied the claimant, who had been contributorily negligent, any compensation would have effectively made him an outlaw. The case was distinguished from a 'joint criminal enterprise', such as *Pitts v Hunt*.

Evans LJ held that it is one thing to deny a claimant any fruits from his illegal conduct, but different, and more far-reaching, to deprive him of compensation for injury which he had suffered and which he was otherwise entitled to recover at law.

The defence of illegality was invoked on grounds of public policy in *Clunis v Camden and Islington Health Authority* [1998]. The claimant, who suffered from a mental illness, attacked and killed a stranger. He sued his health authority in negligence, as they had released him prematurely. This issue was revisited in *Gray v Thames Trains* [2008] in which the defendant sought to recover damages from train company responsible for a crash in which he suffered injury on the basis that it caused him to suffer psychiatric illness that this in turn caused him to kill someone following a traffic altercation. It was held by the House of Lords that he could not recover damages for loss of earnings experienced whilst imprisoned for manslaughter as this was a direct consequence of his unlawful actions.

IMMORAL CONDUCT

Ex turpi applies not only to criminal conduct, but also to immoral conduct. In *Kirkham v Chief Constable of the Greater Manchester Police* [1990], it was said that suicide committed by someone 'wholly sane' would be *ex turpi* but, in that particular case, it did not apply as there was grave mental instability.

However, in *Reeves v Metropolitan Police Commissioner* [1998], the Court of Appeal held that it would be inappropriate to find 'sane suicide' to be *turpis causa*, when Parliament had decriminalised such conduct (Suicide Act 1961). This argument was not pursued on appeal to the House of Lords (1999).

REFORM

The Law Commission's Consultation Paper No 160, *The Illegality Defence in Tort* (2001), provisionally recommends that the defence should be retained, but put on a statutory basis. Courts would be required to consider, as an overarching principle, whether to allow the tort claim to continue would cause inconsistency with other areas of the law (especially criminal law).

MISTAKE

Mistake as to law or to fact is not a general defence. Mistake is not a defence to an intentional tort such as trespass or conversion, however unreasonable.

INEVITABLE ACCIDENT

This used to be a defence in trespass, but now liability in trespass depends upon proof of intention.

However, in negligence, if it can be shown that the accident could not have been avoided by the exercise of reasonable care, then that amounts to a claim that the behaviour was not negligent.

STATUTORY AUTHORITY

A statute may authorise what would otherwise be a tort and an injured party will have no remedy save for that provided by statute.

Statutes often confer powers to act on public and other authorities. Such power will not in general be a defence to a claim in tort.

LIMITATION OF ACTIONS

At common law, there is no limitation period. The rules on limitation are entirely statutory and are now contained in the Limitation Act 1980.

The basic rule is that a claim cannot be brought more than six years from the date the cause of action accrued: s 2 of the Limitation Act 1980.

There are four situations in which different rules apply:

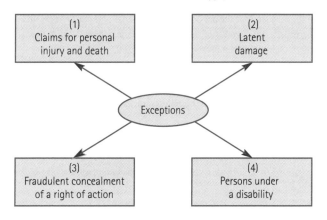

(1) Claims for personal injury and death

In claims for personal injuries, the basic limitation period is three years from either the date on which the cause of action accrued or the date of the claimant's knowledge, whichever is the later (s 11(4) of the Limitation Act 1980).

The court has a wide discretion to disregard this time limit and permit the action to proceed by virtue of s 33 of the Limitation Act 1980.

However, s 11 does not apply to permit the exercise of the discretion in cases of deliberately inflicted injury such as child abuse, see *Stubbings v Webb* [1993] (HL).

The cause of action accrues when the claimant suffers actionable damage irrespective of the claimant's knowledge of the damage, see *Cartledge v E Jobling & Sons Ltd* [1963].

But, the 'date of knowledge' is defined in s 15 of the Limitation Act 1980. The claimant has knowledge of the cause of action when he first has knowledge of the following facts:

- that the injury was significant; and

- that the injury was attributable in whole or in part to the act or omission which is alleged to constitute negligence, nuisance or breach of duty; and

- the identity of the defendant; and

- if it is alleged that the act or omission was that of a person other than the defendant, the identity of that person and the additional facts supporting the bringing of an action against the defendant.

An injury is 'significant' if it would justify proceedings against a defendant who did not dispute liability and was able to satisfy the judgment. Knowledge includes 'constructive knowledge', that is, knowledge a person might reasonably have been expected to acquire.

After a major operation, the date of knowledge for the purposes of s 11 of the Limitation Act 1980 occurs as soon as the claimant has had time to overcome the shock of the injury, take stock of his disability and seek advice (*Forbes v Wandsworth HA* [1996]).

With regard to the discretion given by s 33, the court will have regard to all the circumstances, and the exercise of the discretion is something of a lottery. The discretion was held to be unfettered in *Firman v Ellis* [1978].

By s 33(3), the court must have regard to particular aspects of the matter: for example, the length of and reasons for the delay; the defendant's conduct; the effect of delay on the evidence; the claimant's conduct, etc.

In deciding whether to exercise its discretion to disapply the three year rule under s 33 of the Limitation Act 1980, the court should apply a subjective rather than an objective test as to the reasons for the claimant's delay in instituting proceedings (*Coad v Cornwall and Isles of Scilly HA* [1997]).

A subjective test was again applied in *Spargo v North Essex District Health Authority* [1997].

(2) Latent damage

Where damage is latent, the claimant will be unaware that the damage has actually occurred. As a result, the cause of action may accrue and become statute barred before the claimant even knows about the damage or his right to sue.

> ### ▶ CARTLEDGE v E JOBLING & SONS LTD [1963]
>
> Basic facts
> The claimant contracted pneumoconiosis from the inhalation of dust over a long period of working in a particular environment. The damage to the lungs was latent and the claimant was unaware of it.
>
> Relevance
> The House of Lords held that the cause of action accrued when significant damage to the lungs occurred, and it was irrelevant whether the claimant knew of the damage or not. As a result of this decision, the law of limitation was changed by statute in relation to personal injuries.

This left the problem of what to do about defective buildings. Various tests for the commencement of the limitation period were developed. For example:

- some felt the limitation period should begin with the date of construction;

- others felt that time should run when the claimant discovered the damage or ought reasonably to have done so.

However, in *Pirelli General Cable Works Ltd v Oscar Faber & Partners* [1983] it was held that the action accrued, and therefore the limitation period commenced, when physical damage to the building actually occurred, regardless of whether it could be discovered by the claimant. A distinction is thus made between structural fault and the defect arising from it.

Pirelli caused one or two problems. The Latent Damage Act 1986 tried to redress the problem. It introduced a special extension of the limitation period in respect of latent damage (other than physical injury) and it gives the claimant three years from the date on which he discovered significant damage. This amends the Limitation Act accordingly. All claims are subject to an absolute bar for claims for 15 years from the date of the defendant's negligence.

Murphy v Brentwood District Council [1990] authoritatively classified the loss in building cases as pure economic loss, and not physical damage – simply, the defective building is less valuable than it should have been. Thus, in New Zealand, the damage happens (and the action accrues) when it is discovered, since this is when the loss in economic value comes about, see *Invercargill City Council v Hamlin* [1996]. This logical approach would avoid the need for the Latent Damage Act altogether. However, the Court of Appeal has recently confirmed that, however illogical, *Pirelli* remains good law, unless reconsidered in terms by the House of Lords.

Thus, in England, damage still accrues when physical changes occur, see *Abbott v Will Gannon & Smith Ltd* [2005].

Although there is still a duty owed by builders to the owners of a dwelling, in s 1 of the Defective Premises Act 1972, it was held in *Payne v John Setchell* [2001] that the Latent Damage Act 1986 applies only to common law negligence and does not assist actions under the Act of 1972.

(3) Fraudulent concealment of a right of action

Where the defendant has deliberately concealed from the claimant the facts of a tort, the period of limitation does not commence until the claimant has discovered the fraud or could with reasonable diligence have done so.

Therefore, in *Kitchen v Royal Air Force Association* [1958], a failure by solicitors to inform the claimant of an offer of £100 by potential defendants, because that might reveal their own negligence at an earlier stage, constituted deliberate concealment.

(4) Persons under a disability

Time does not run against an infant, or a person of unsound mind, until he ceases to be under a disability or dies, whichever occurs.

However, if the claimant was not under a disability when the action accrued but subsequently becomes of unsound mind, this will not prevent time from running.

You should now be confident that you would be able to tick all of the boxes on the checklist at the beginning of this chapter. To check your knowledge of General defences why not visit the companion website and take the Multiple Choice Question test. Check your understanding of the terms and vocabulary used in this chapter with the flashcard glossary.

Remedies

What is the aim of compensation in tort?	
What are the different heads of damage and when are they awarded?	
How are damages calculated in personal injury claims?	
Is the claimant under a duty to mitigate their losses?	

Remedies in tort are concerned with two main aims. Depending on the specific tort that has been committed, claimants are likely to want either to obtain financial compensation for the loss or injury that they have suffered (damages) or to prevent the continuation or recurrence of the problem that has occurred (injunction). It should be remembered that a particular incident may give rise to various forms of remedy of which tortious remedies form only part. For instance, many claimants will be compensated via insurance payouts from the defendant without the matter ever having to go to court. There are also schemes relating to criminal injuries compensation and various systems of state compensation and benefits.

AIMS OF COMPENSATION

The aim of tort compensation is to restore the claimant to the position he would have been in had the tort not been committed: *Livingstone v Rawyards Coal Co* [1880].

It has been argued that the compensation system is based on the wrong principles. The claimant is compensated for what he has actually lost. The defendant is therefore liable for a greater amount of damages if he injures a high-earning claimant as opposed to a low-earning claimant. It has been said that damages should be based on what the claimant needs rather than on what he has lost. This is particularly relevant in cases of severe injury.

Further criticisms are based on the guesswork involved in calculating future loss and that compensation depends on the fault principle. Both of these points are considered in greater depth below.

A SINGLE CLAIM AND LUMP SUM

A claimant can bring only one claim in respect of a single wrong. He cannot maintain a second claim based on the same facts merely because the damage turns out to be more extensive than was anticipated. He can recover damages once only and the cause of the action is extinguished by the claim. The authority for this is *Fetter v Beale* [1701], in which the claimant failed in his claim for further damages after his medical condition deteriorated following his first award of damages.

If one and the same act violates two rights which are accorded separate protection by tort law, there are two separate causes of action, and the prosecution of one will not bar proceedings in respect of the other.

In *Brunsden v Humphrey* [1884], a cab driven by the claimant collided with the defendant's van through the negligent driving of the defendant's servant. In county court proceedings, the claimant recovered compensation for damage to his cab. He then brought a second action in the High Court for personal injuries sustained by him in the same collision, and the Court of Appeal held that this action was not barred by the earlier one.

Damages are assessed once and for all and can be awarded in the form of a lump sum or, since 1989, as a structured settlement, whereby the damages are divided into a lump sum and periodic payments (see below). This 'once and for all' principle causes difficulties where loss in the future is uncertain. In personal injury claims, the claimant's medical condition may become much worse or much better than expected. In the words of Lord Scarman in *Lim Poh Choo v Camden and Islington AHA* [1979]:

> Knowledge of the future being denied to mankind, so much of the award as is attributed to future loss and suffering will almost surely be wrong. There is only one certainty: the future will prove the award to be either too high or too low.

DISADVANTAGES OF LUMP SUM SYSTEM
A number of criticisms have been made of the lump sum system. These can be identified as follows:

(1) Lump sums do not fulfil the aims of tort compensation
The aim of tort damages is to place the claimant in the position he would have been in if the tort had not been committed. A lump sum carries with it the responsibility of investment, to ensure future income from the lump sum. If the claimant were to be truly compensated for his loss then he would receive a regular income in place of his lost earnings.

(2) Lump sums are easily dissipated
There is nothing preventing the claimant from spending the lump sum before the end of the period for which it was intended that he would be compensated.

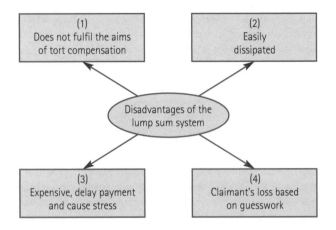

This would leave the claimant potentially reliant upon state benefits and thus being doubly compensated for a single injury.

(3) Lump sums are expensive, delay payment and cause stress

As lump sums are a once and for all system of compensation, they tend to encourage delay prior to settlement. There is every incentive to wait until the claimant's condition has stabilised, as much as possible, to ensure that the quantum of damages reflects the claimant's loss as closely as possible. Because an assessment of the claimant's future condition involves guesswork, reliance is placed on expert reports, which frequently conflict and this increases delay and costs. There is little incentive for the defendant to settle early. The claimant may be in receipt of welfare payments which may pressurise him into settling early and for too little. A medical condition termed 'compensation neurosis' has been identified, whereby the claimant's condition fails to improve pending the outcome of the case. In addition, once the case has been settled, the claimant has to manage a sum which is probably greater than any other he has had to deal with in his life, and also ensure that it lasts for the rest of his life.

(4) Lump sums are based on guesswork

A number of projections have to be made when assessing the claimant's loss under the lump sum system: his future condition, his future earning prospects, his promotion prospects prior to the accident, etc. A lump sum system does not allow for a change in circumstance, whereas a system of periodic payments allows for occasional review.

TYPES OF DAMAGES

NOMINAL DAMAGES

Nominal damages are awarded where the claimant has proved his case but has suffered no loss: *Constantine v Imperial Hotels Ltd* [1944]. The claimant will be awarded only a small amount of money. Nominal damages can be awarded only for those torts which are actionable *per se*.

CONTEMPTUOUS DAMAGES

Contemptuous damages are awarded where the claim is technically successful but is without merit and the claim should not have been brought. The amount of damages is usually the smallest coin in the realm. The judge will normally order the claimant to pay his own costs, and may even order him to pay the defendant's costs as well.

AGGRAVATED DAMAGES

Aggravated damages are compensatory. They are awarded where the claimant has suffered more than can reasonably be expected in the situation. They will be awarded where the claimant's proper feelings of dignity and pride have been injured, see *Jolliffe v Willmett & Co* [1971]. They have also been awarded where the tort was committed in a malicious, insulting or oppressive manner, see *Broome v Cassell & Co Ltd* [1972]. They will not be awarded in cases of personal injury where the tort was committed in a way that was more painful than necessary, as a higher award for pain and suffering will reflect this, see *Kralj v McGrath* [1986]; *AB v South West Water Services Ltd* [1993].

The Law Commission in its 1997 Report, *Aggravated, Exemplary and Restitutionary Damages*, recommended that aggravated damages should be re-named 'damages for mental distress' to make it clear that they are compensatory.

EXEMPLARY DAMAGES

Exemplary damages are intended to be punitive and can therefore be distinguished from aggravated damages which are compensatory. They take the form of an additional award on top of the compensatory award. They are an exception to the rule that the aim of damages in tort is to compensate. They are unpopular with judges as exemplary damages confuse the aims of the criminal and civil law, and it is also thought undesirable to punish a defendant without the safeguards inherent in the criminal law. By contrast, it has been argued, most notably by Lord Wilberforce in *Broome v Cassell & Co Ltd* [1972], that tort has a deterrent function in addition to a compensatory function, and that exemplary damages are therefore a legitimate part of the compensation system. Nevertheless, a restrictive approach has been taken, and it was held in *Rookes v Barnard* [1964] that exemplary damages could be awarded only in three situations:

- Oppressive, arbitrary or unconstitutional action by servants of government. The term 'servants of government' includes police officers and also local and central government officials. It was held in *AB v South West Water Services Ltd* [1993] that publicly-owned utilities which provide a monopoly service are outside the category. A man who had been seriously assaulted by police officers was entitled to substantial exemplary damages, and these damages were not reduced on the grounds of his serious previous convictions in *Treadaway v Chief Constable of West Midlands* [1994].

- Where the defendant's conduct has been calculated to make a profit for himself which exceeds the compensation payable. In *Broome v Cassell & Co Ltd* [1972], the defendants published a book which they knew contained defamatory statements about the claimant. They believed that the increased profits from the sale would exceed any award of damages. £15,000 compensatory damages were awarded, with an additional £25,000 exemplary damages. In *AB v South West Water Services Ltd* [1993], covering up the existence of a tort did not come within this category.

- Where statute authorises the award of exemplary damages. In *Kuddus v Chief Constable of Leicestershire* [2001], the House of Lords held (overruling *AB v South West Water* on this point) that there was no rule that exemplary damages could be recovered only in torts where they had been recovered prior to the decision in *Rookes v Barnard* [1964]. Thus, they could be awarded for the tort of misfeasance in public office (which had not been recognised in 1964). It was recognised that this amounted to an extension of the heads of exemplary damages (an extension criticised by Lord Scott as 'regrettable').

The Court of Appeal laid down guidelines to juries for the award of exemplary damages against the police in *Thompson v Commissioner of Police of the Metropolis* [1997]. It is unlikely to be less than £5,000 and might be as much as £25,000 where an officer of the rank of superintendent or above is involved.

The Law Commission in its 1997 Report, *Aggravated, Exemplary and Restitutionary Damages*, recommended that exemplary damages be re-named 'punitive damages'. A judge, as opposed to a jury, should recommend whether they are awardable and their amount. Defendants should be liable to pay them for any tort or equitable wrong, or a civil wrong arising under statute, in any case where the defendant's behaviour in committing the wrong, or after it has been committed, deliberately or outrageously disregarded the claimant's rights.

GENERAL AND SPECIAL DAMAGE

There are two meanings to these terms. First, general damage can mean the damage that is presumed to flow from torts which are actionable *per se*, for example, trespass; and special damage is the damage the claimant must prove where damage is an element of the tort, for example, negligence.

The second and more common meaning is that general damages are those which cannot be calculated precisely, whereas special damages are those which can be calculated precisely at the date of trial.

DAMAGES IN PERSONAL INJURY CLAIMS

A claimant who suffers injuries incurs two types of loss: pecuniary loss, for example, loss of earnings, expenses, etc; and non-pecuniary loss, for example, pain and suffering or loss of a limb.

(1) Medical and other expenses

Under s 2(4) of the Law Reform (Personal Injuries) Act 1948, the claimant may incur private medical expenses and recover the same, despite the availability of the NHS. The Pearson Commission recommended that private medical expenses should be recoverable only where it was reasonable that they should be incurred on medical grounds, but this proposal has not been implemented.

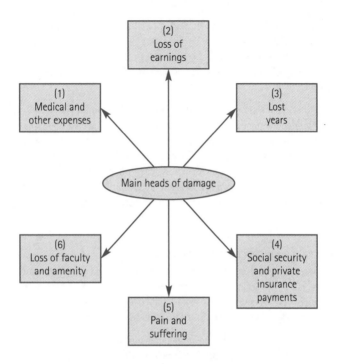

Section 5 of the Administration of Justice Act 1982 provides that where an injured person makes a saving by being maintained at public expense in a hospital, nursing home or other institution, then such saving must be set off against his loss of income. The Road Traffic (NHS Charges) Act 1999 enables NHS hospitals to recover the cost of treating accident victims from defendants' insurers.

If the claimant has to change to special accommodation as a result of his injuries then the additional annual cost over ordinary accommodation is recoverable. The cost of adapting accommodation or a car to special needs is also recoverable. The capital cost of special accommodation or car is not recoverable as it is an asset which belongs to the claimant.

An example of an additional expense incurred as a result of a tort is contained in *Jones v Jones* [1984]. The claimant's injuries led to the breakdown of his marriage. The Court of Appeal held that the extra cost to the claimant of having to finance two homes instead of one was, in principle, recoverable. This case has been criticised on the basis that it is not felt that marriage breakdown is really foreseeable. By contrast, it was held in *Pritchard v JH Cobden Ltd* [1987] that the cost of a marriage breakdown caused by injuries was not recoverable either because it was too remote or on grounds that it was contrary to public policy.

In *Donnelly v Joyce* [1973], the claimant's loss included the cost incurred by a third party. For example, where a relative or friend provides nursing assistance or financial assistance, then this can be catered for in the claimant's claim. Where a relative has given up work then the loss of earnings will be recoverable, provided they do not exceed the commercial cost of nursing care, see *Housecroft v Burnett* [1986].

(2) Loss of earnings

This can be divided into:

- actual loss; and

- future loss.

Actual loss runs from the date of the accident to the date of assessment (settlement or trial). It is not permissible to profit from loss of earnings, so income tax and social security contributions must be deducted in order to ascertain the net loss, see *British Transport Commission v Gourley* [1955]. Loss of perks, for example, a company car, is also taken into account.

Future loss is speculative and relates to losses the claimant will suffer after the date of assessment.

First, it is necessary to calculate the net loss of earnings; this is known as the multiplicand. Secondly, tax and social security contributions are deducted from the claimant's earnings to arrive at the net figure. Lastly, the multiplicand is adjusted to take account of future promotion prospects.

The multiplicand is multiplied by an appropriate multiplier up to a maximum of 18. In practice, the multiplier is rarely this high as it is discounted to take account of future uncertainties and also accelerated receipt. The sum awarded which is invested should provide for lost earnings, the claimant being expected to live off the investment income and part of the capital. Future inflation is not taken into account as that should be covered by shrewd investment. In cases of very large awards, the House of Lords held in *Hodgson v Trapp* [1988] that the multiplier could not be increased to reflect the fact that the claimant would be paying tax at higher tax levels.

There has been a flurry of case law concerning the multiplier. At first instance, in *Wells v Wells* [1998]; *Thomas v Brighton Health Authority* [1995]; and *Page v Sheerness Steel Co plc* [1998], the judge fixed the multiplier by reference to the return on index-linked government securities at 3 per cent per year. These are safe investments, involving minimum risk. The effect was to make the multiplier significantly higher and the damages were greatly increased.

All three cases were heard together in the Court of Appeal in 1996, where it was held that the assumption in large awards was that the claimant would seek advice on how to manage the money. A basket of investments would include a substantial proportion of riskier equities as well as index-linked government securities (ILGS). Consequently, the conventional discount rate of 4.5 per cent continued to apply.

When the joined appeals reached the House of Lords in 1998, it was accepted that it must be assumed that investment will be based on ILGS. However, a prudent investment would be based on a balanced portfolio which would include some riskier equities. The House of Lords held that the rate of return (and hence discount) should be based on ILGS giving an average return of 3 per cent. Consequently, the awards in the cases were raised. It is believed that this decision has been responsible for a series of very high awards of damages after July 1998 in cases involving long-term future care.

In *Warren v Northern General Hospital* [2000], the Court of Appeal refused to reduce the 3 per cent rate yet further, despite the further decrease in returns on ILGS. They held that it was for the Lord Chancellor to set the rate, using powers under the Damages Act 1996. They further held that the impact of taxation on a large fund did not justify application of a rate different from that in *Wells v Wells*. Subsequently, the Lord Chancellor reduced the rate to 2.5 per cent, in the Damages (Personal Injury) Order 2001. In 2002, the Lord Chancellor's Department (now Department for Constitutional Affairs) estimated the annual cost of this change at £169 million.

(3) 'Lost years'

Where the claimant's life expectancy has been reduced as a result of his injuries, the question is whether he can be compensated for the earnings he would have received between the date of his expected death and the date he would have stopped working if the accident had not occurred.

It was held in *Oliver v Ashman* [1961] that claims for the lost years were not recoverable.

The House of Lords overruled *Oliver v Ashman* in *Pickett v British Rail Engineering* [1979], and damages for prospective loss of earnings are now awarded for the whole of the claimant's pre-accident life expectancy, subject to deduction of his living expenses.

(4) Social security and private insurance payments

Some social security payments are deducted from the claimant's loss of income. Section 22 of the Social Security Act 1989, which is now incorporated into the Social Security Administration Act 1992, enables welfare payments made to the claimant to be recouped from the defendant. The system was amended by the Social Security (Recovery of Benefits) Act 1997. The full value of all recoverable benefits during the relevant period (applying to all settlements and judgments after 6 October 1997) must be deducted before payment from the claimant's damages. The defendant cannot pay the damages award until he has obtained a certificate of the benefits paid or payable, and recovered the same from the award.

Private insurance payments are not deducted as the defendant would thereby profit from the claimant's foresight. Payments made under an accident insurance policy taken out by an employer on behalf of employees are also nondeductible, see *McCamley v Cammell Laird Shipbuilders Ltd* [1990]. *Ex gratia* payments made by a charity are also not deductible. An occupational disability pension is not deducted, see *Parry v Cleaver* [1969]. This was affirmed in *Smoker v London Fire and Civil Defence Authority* [1991] on the basis that a pension is deferred payment. Occupational sick pay will be deducted, see *Hussain v New Taplow Paper Mills Ltd* [1988].

In *Longdon v British Coal Corporation* [1997], the House of Lords held that an incapacity pension awarded before normal retirement age should not be deducted.

(5) Pain and suffering

The claimant is entitled to be compensated for actual and prospective pain and suffering. Section 1(1)(b) of the Administration of Justice Act 1982 allows a claimant who knows that his life expectancy has been reduced to recover for that anguish. A permanently unconscious claimant cannot claim for pain and suffering, see *Wise v Kaye* [1962].

(6) Loss of faculty and amenity

A tariff system of £X for the loss of a leg and £Y for the loss of an arm exists. Refer to *Kemp and Kemp: The Quantum of Damages* for details. Loss of amenity involves the lost chances to use the faculty. Loss of amenity will be greater for a keen sportsman who loses a leg than a couch potato who spends his life watching TV.

The award of loss of amenity is made objectively, see, for example, *H West & Sons Ltd v Shephard* [1963], where the claimant was unconscious and unable to appreciate his condition.

In *Heil v Rankin* [2000], a five-member Court of Appeal held that there should be an across-the-board, tapered increase in damages for pain, suffering and loss of amenity. Damages of £150,000 were to be increased by 33 per cent; those of £110,000 by 25 per cent; those of £80,000 by 20 per cent; and awards of £40,000 by 10 per cent. This was in accordance with the suggestions contained in Law Commission Report No 257 (1999), and was said to be a 'modest increase' necessary to keep awards fair, reasonable and just.

NEW METHODS OF PAYING DAMAGES IN PERSONAL INJURY CASES

STRUCTURED SETTLEMENTS

For many years, damages were assessed once and paid in one lump sum payment (see above). The rule that damages are assessed once still applies, but since the case of *Kelly v Dawes* [1990], payments can be made in the form of periodic payments known as structured settlements. These were first introduced in the United States and Canada, where they are further advanced. Their inception in this country was made possible by the Inland Revenue agreeing that periodic payments were payment of capital and not income, which had certain tax advantages.

The system works with the lump sum being calculated in the conventional way. Part of the lump sum is paid over to the claimant immediately. The rest of the payment is used to purchase an annuity from an insurer with payments being structured over a given period, which can be for the claimant's lifetime or longer if the claimant has dependants.

ADVANTAGES OF STRUCTURED SETTLEMENTS

The main advantage is that the periodic payments are free of tax in the claimant's hands. The payments are treated by the Inland Revenue as an 'antecedent debt', and are therefore treated as capital rather than income and are not subject to income tax. Contrast this with the investment income from a lump sum which is subject to income tax.

There are also financial advantages for the defendant's insurer. As structures involve the insurer in greater administration costs, they also argue that they are entitled to a share of the resulting tax benefits to the claimant, and they are able to negotiate a discount on the lump sum, which is usually in the range of 8–15 per cent. It has been argued that a discount in excess of 8 per cent makes structured settlements unattractive as they are likely to be out-performed by investments. This view has been criticised on the grounds that it overlooks the value of the certainty the claimant has in knowing that his periodic payments are secure.

They are useful in cases where the claimant would be unable to manage a lump sum payment. They also lead to the claimant escaping the management and investment costs of investing a lump sum. This better reflects the situation the claimant would have been in if the tort had not been committed than a lump sum payment, as a regular income avoids the stress of financial management and does not need the presence of financial experts to ensure its continuance.

The income derived from the annuity is protected from the vagaries of the inflation rate or wild fluctuations in the stock market.

There is flexibility in the creation of the structure. The parties can decide the proportion of the lump sum payment that is to go into an immediate capital payment and how much is to go into the structure.

It ensures that the payments will not cease during the claimant's lifetime. A lump sum payment can be dissipated by the claimant either through his being

145

spendthrift, or through ill-advised investment or because a prognosis as to life expectancy proves to be incorrect, with the claimant living longer than has been anticipated. Regardless of the manner in which the dissipation occurs, the claimant will become a charge on the state when it is the aim of the compensation system to avoid this happening.

In Consultation Paper No 125, the Law Commission identified other advantages of the system as encouraging early settlement, thereby saving time and costs and providing certainty for the claimant. Early settlement reduces the stress of the litigation process which has proved to be harmful to claimants' rehabilitation.

As settlements provide the claimant with an income, they better fulfil the aims of compensation compared to a lump sum payment, as they actually substitute what the claimant has lost. They provide income in place of lost earnings.

An advantage for the state is that the defendant is much less likely to claim welfare benefit. A settlement also creates less pressure on the legal system as it promotes early settlement of claims and ensures that the compensation is used for the purpose for which it is intended.

It improves the image of the compensation system. Instead of the insurer handing over a lump sum to the claimant and washing his hands entirely of the case, the replacement system ensures that provision is made for the rest of the claimant's life. In this sense, it is a more humane system.

Disadvantages of structured settlements
As the amount of the structure is assessed only once, it does not solve the guesswork involved in the assessment of damages. In its Consultation Paper the Law Commission said: 'The pressure to get it right at an early stage is extreme.' It is still possible for the amount of damages to prove inadequate due to an incorrect prognosis. The Pearson Commission recommended a system of structured settlements which would be reviewed in the light of deteriorating financial circumstances. This would get round some of the problems relating to guesswork, but the proposal has not been adopted. To a certain extent, all compensatory systems are subject to a certain amount of guesswork. Even a fully reviewable system of periodic payments still has to be based on assumptions relating to promotion prospects, etc.

A further disadvantage is that the operation of the structure is not very flexible. Once the structure is established, it cannot be changed. If there is unforeseen demand for capital, the structure will not be able to accommodate this need. This contrasts with the degree of flexibility which exists at the time the structure is created, when the parties can decide how much will be given in immediate capital payment and how much will go into the structure. For a minority of claimants, the loss of freedom and discretion as to the manner in which the lump sum should be invested is a serious disadvantage.

At one time, the claimant was subject to the risk that the insurer could become insolvent. Following the Law Commission's Report No 224, the claimant is now protected from failure of the life office. Structured settlements have been brought within the Policyholders Protection Act 1975. The Secretary of State can guarantee 'directly funded' settlements such as those by NHS trusts.

The system may simply replace 'compensation neurosis' with a different form of neurosis. The claimant may perceive his dependency on the monthly cheque as making his position analogous to that of a welfare recipient.

The system increases administrative costs and imposes a long-term financial obligation on the defendant.

If the question is looked at in its wider context then it can be seen that, as tort victims are already generously compensated in comparison to those who receive compensation outside the tort system, the system, in the words of Michael Jones, makes an 'elite group even more elite'.

Structured settlements do not alter the fact that the system is predicated on compensating the claimant for what he has lost rather than on what he needs. By alleviating some of the difficulties associated with the lump sum system, structured settlements may simply be postponing a more fundamental reform of the compensation system.

Limits to structured settlements

Structures cannot be used in all cases and certain limits have been placed upon them.

Both parties must consent to the structure. It was held in *Burke v Tower Hamlets AHA* [1989] that the defendant could not be made to make periodic payments against its wishes.

A structure cannot be imposed after the parties have formally agreed settlement or obtained judgment for a certain sum.

To preserve a structure where a case goes to trial, s 2 of the Damages Act 1996 enables the court with the consent of both parties to make an award under which damages are wholly or partly paid by periodic payments.

A structure cannot be imposed where provisional damages are sought, nor where interim damages have been awarded.

It cannot be used in very small claims as administrative costs make it uneconomic.

Structured settlements cannot be used where there is no liability, for example, awards made by the Criminal Injuries Compensation Board (CICB), despite their decisions being subject to judicial review.

So far, structures have been awarded only in cases of personal injury involving very high awards of damages, and it is doubtful whether they will be extended into other areas. Structured settlements are now used much less frequently than in the past. Several reasons have been suggested for this, including the House of Lords' decision in *Wells v Wells*, the global economic climate, and radical changes in procedure and practice in civil cases introduced in 1999.

Structures are not available for special damages but are reserved specifically for general damages, that is, those damages which cannot be calculated precisely, including future loss.

DAMAGE TO PROPERTY

Where property is completely destroyed, the measure of damages is the market value of the property at the time of destruction.

Further losses flowing from property damage may be recoverable if foreseeable. In *Liesbosch Dredger v SS Edison* [1933], the claimants' dredger was destroyed through the defendants' negligence. The claimants suffered heavy consequential losses since they were unable to perform their contract with the local Harbour Commissioners. However, these consequential losses were said not to be recoverable; they were held to be solely attributable to the claimants' impecuniosity, which meant that they were unable to hire a replacement vessel to continue performance of the contract.

More recently, hire costs have been allowed in *Martindale v Duncan* [1973], and in *Motor Works Ltd v Alwahbi* [1977] it was reasonable for the claimant to hire a Rolls-Royce while his own Rolls-Royce was being repaired.

Where property is damaged but not destroyed, the measure of damages is the diminution in value, normally the cost of repair.

MITIGATION OF LOSS

A claimant has a duty to mitigate the damage that results from the defendant's tort. But no wrong is committed against the defendant if he fails to do so. In *Darbishire v Warran* [1963], it was said that the claimant was 'entitled to be as extravagant as he pleases but not at the expense of the defendant'.

INJUNCTIONS

An injunction is an equitable remedy and is, therefore, discretionary. A prohibitory injunction is an order of the court requiring the defendant to cease committing a continuing tort. As an equitable remedy, it will not be awarded if damages would be an adequate remedy.

Mandatory injunctions are not granted as readily as prohibitory injunctions; there must be a strong probability that very serious damage to the claimant will result if withheld.

You should now be confident that you would be able to tick all of the boxes on the checklist at the beginning of this chapter. To check your knowledge of Remedies why not visit the companion website and take the Multiple Choice Question test. Check your understanding of the terms and vocabulary used in this chapter with the flashcard glossary.

7

Putting it into practice...

Now that you've mastered the basics, you will want to put it all into practice. The Routledge Questions and Answers series provides an ideal opportunity for you to apply your understanding and knowledge of the law and to hone your essay-writing technique.

We've included one exam-style essay question, which replicates the type of question posed in the Routledge Questions and Answers series to give you some essential exam practice. The Q&A includes an answer plan and a fully worked model answer to help you recognise what examiners might look for in your answer.

QUESTION 1

Factor X (FX), an events management company, was contracted to provide corporate hospitality by Womberfield Stadium for clients attending a sporting event. In order to exclude the general public from the exclusive corporate hospitality area, FX engaged its usual contactors, Crew Service (CS), to provide security for the day in question. The security staff's instructions from FX were detailed and included a specific instruction not to admit people without a ticket, along with an instruction that should there be any problem with a non-ticket holder trying to enter, the member of staff should radio a member of FX staff and wait for them to attend to resolve the situation.

The centrepiece to the hospitality buffet was an elaborate chocolate fountain. Paula, an FX employee, assembled the fountain incorrectly and did not test it as she had been instructed to do. As a result of the incorrect assembly, the fountain later toppled over, scalding several guests and knocking one unconscious. During the commotion, Scally tried to sneak into the event but was caught by Louie, one of the security staff. Louie violently twisted Scally's arm and threw him to the ground, breaking Scally's wrist and cutting his head.

Answer Plan

This question involves a consideration of the principles of vicarious liability in situations in which an employee has been negligent and also those in which the employee has committed a wilful act. It also involves the question of who may be held to be an employer in cases in which there is more than one possibility.

The following points require discussion:

- the liability of Paula to the guests;

- the liability of an employer for the negligence of employee;

- the basics of the tort of battery;

- the liability of an employer for deliberate torts committed by an employee;

- determining the employer for the purposes of liability.

ANSWER

This question requires an application of the laws relating to vicarious liability – that is, making an employer liable for the tortious acts of his employees. As a result of Paula's failure to assemble the machinery correctly, people have been injured, and it first falls to be determined whether they could sue Paula and, if so, whether FX can be held vicariously liable. There should be no problem in demonstrating that Paula owed a duty of care. To determine the existence of a duty of care since the case of *Caparo Industries plc v Dickman* [1990] requires a consideration of the reasonable foreseeability of harm, the proximity of the relationship between the claimant and defendant, and whether it is fair, just and reasonable to impose the duty on the defendant. In the circumstances, it is highly probably that Paula owes a duty of care, as it is foreseeable that improper assembly and a lack of testing of the fountain could lead to damage, the proximity requirement is satisfied, and it is fair, just and reasonable to impose such a duty. It has also been noted (*B v Islington Health Authority* [1991]) that as far as personal injury cases are concerned, the duty remains as it was pre-*Caparo* – namely, the foresight of a reasonable person (*Donoghue v Stevenson* [1932]).

Whether Paula was in breach of that duty depends upon an assessment of the reasonableness of her conduct: in other words, would a reasonable person have behaved in the way that she did (*Blyth v Birmingham Waterworks* [1856])? Given the facts, it is unlikely that she has performed to the required standard and is therefore in breach of her duty. Next, the guests would have to demonstrate that her breach of duty caused their injuries. The basic approach is to utilise the 'but for' test (*Barnett v Chelsea and Kensington Hospital Management Committee* [1969]), essentially meaning: but for the defendant's breach of duty, would the damage have occurred? Once again, the linkage is simple and can easily be attributed to Paula's negligence. Finally, it must be determined whether the damage suffered was too remote a consequence of the breach (*The Wagon*

Mound (No 1) [1961]) – in other words, was the damage of a type or kind that was reasonably foreseeable? In this case, all that would need to be shown would be that personal injury was reasonably foreseeable. Clearly it was. Paula is therefore very likely to be held to have been negligent.

Can FX be held liable for Paula's negligence? To be vicariously liable, Paula must be an employee of FX. We are told that she is. Next it must be shown that Paula is acting in the course of her employment. The basic test is to determine whether her act was something that was a wrongful or unauthorised manner of doing an authorised act, or whether it was so far removed from what was authorised as to be independent from it (*Century Insurance v Northern Ireland Road Transport Board* [1942]; *Lister v Helsey Hall* [2001]). A contemporary application can be seen in *Grauil v Carroll* [2008] where a rugby club was held liable for one of its players punching an opponent in the face. Paula was clearly in the course of her employment while setting up the chocolate fountain; the fact that she did so wrongly, or in an unauthorised manner, is not sufficient to enable FX to escape liability for her conduct. Accordingly, the advice to the injured guests would be to sue FX for the damage that they have suffered.

As far as Louie is concerned, it is likely that he has committed battery, an element of the tort of trespass to the person. Battery is defined as a direct, intentional application of force by the defendant in the absence of the claimant's consent. The force must be direct (*Reynolds v Clarke* [1725]) and intentional (*Letang v Cooper* [1965]), so in the circumstances, Scally would have little trouble in proving these elements. Additionally, any form of touching or application of force is capable of being a battery (*Cole v Turner* [1704]): clearly, an arm twist and being thrown to the ground would suffice. There is an element of uncertainty as to whether the touching should be hostile or not (*Wilson v Pringle* [1987]; *F v West Berkshire Health Authority* [1989]), but irrespective of that debate, there would be no problem in establishing a battery in this situation as the touching is undoubtedly hostile and falls well within the description of the tort. There would also be little chance of Louie being able to claim that he was acting in self-defence, as that particular defence would require that the force used was reasonable (*Turner v MGM* [1950]; *Cross v Kirkby* [2000]); additionally, the defence of protecting a third party's property is also limited by the same requirement. Louie, it would appear, has definitely committed the tort of battery; he is also likely to have committed a criminal offence for which he could be charged, but it would be in Scally's interests to seek to sue Louie's employer for the tortious act. The case of *Majrowski v Guy's & St Thomas' NHS Trust* [2006] has extended an employer's liability to harassment, under the Protection from Harassment Act 1997, committed by an employee in the course of his employment.

It now falls to consider whether Louie's employer could be held vicariously liable for his battery. The question to be determined is whether an employer can be held liable for the deliberate torts of an employee. Previously, the law sought to establish a link between the act of the employee and the nature of the employment that s/he was engaged in, or that there was attributable fault on the part of the employer, for example by not supervising the employee closely enough (*Lloyd v Grace, Smith & Co* [1912]; *Warren v Henley's Ltd* [1948]). More recently, in *Lister v Helsey Hall* [2001], the House of Lords was asked to determine whether an employer, a boys' school, could be held vicariously liable for a series of sexual abuses perpetrated by one of its wardens. It was held that it could. The test according to the Lords was whether the nature of the employment was close to the wrongdoing perpetrated by the employee. Departing from earlier authority, the House of Lords held that there was no need for the tort to be committed in the furtherance of the employer's business. A similar case, involving an assault by a doorman at a nightclub, was also upheld against the employer in *Mattis v Pollock* [2003] and see also *Hawley v Luminar Leisure Ltd* [2006], considered further below. It would therefore appear that an employer could be liable for Louie's actions, but the question remains, which one?

Louie is employed by CS; however, it would appear from the facts that he has been 'lent' to FX by virtue of the fact that FX has hired in security from CS. In such circumstances, you would perhaps think that the contract between the two companies would be decisive on the issue. Case law, however, has suggested that it is not that simple. In *Mersey Docks and Harbour Board v Coggins and Griffiths* [1947], the appellants lent a crane driver and crane to the respondents. Due to the crane driver's negligence, a third party suffered personal injury and it was therefore necessary to determine which employer was vicariously liable. The contract between the parties indicated that the hirer was liable, but the House of Lords held that in such circumstances the contract could not decide the issue. Instead, it created a presumption that the permanent employer would be liable unless it could overcome the burden of proving otherwise, which it could not. Two recent decisions appear to have altered that position. In

Viasystems Ltd v Thermal Transfer Ltd [2005], the Court of Appeal reviewed vicarious liability and concluded that the decision as to whether an employee remained an employee of the permanent employer, or was 'deemed to be the temporary employee of the hirer of his services', turned on the question of control. In that case, it was held that more than one employer could be vicariously liable, although that would depend on the facts of the case and in particular the integration of the employee into the business of both employers. The judgment was approved in *Hawley*, in which a nightclub doorman seriously assaulted a person outside a club. It was held that the nightclub was vicariously liable for his actions, even though he was deemed a temporary employee. Applying *Viasystems* and *Hawley* to the situation involving Louie, it would appear that FX may well be vicariously liable as it issued instructions and could be said to have control over the performance of the task; failing that, there is the possibility that both employers might share liability to Scally.

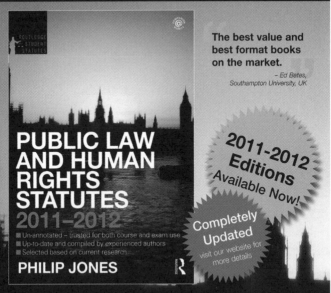